The Franchisee Handbook is jam packed with great advice to help steer prospective franchisees into making a well-informed decision as to which opportunity might suit them best and, more importantly, helping them avoid opportunities that are not a good fit.

—SETH BRINK, GYRO SHACK

Having worked with Mark ⋯ ⋯ ties, I know how important it is for fr⋯ ⋯ they are getting into before they buy. This ⋯ ⋯ chisees with a great roadmap to guide the⋯ ⋯ g one of the biggest financial de⋯⋯⋯ they will ever make.

—TOM RYAN, VICE PRESIDENT OF DEVELOPMENT, CD ONE PRICE CLEANERS

As both a franchisee and as a franchisor, I can attest to Mark's philosophy that there is nothing more important than ensuring the franchisee and franchisor are a good fit for each other. The lessons in this book should be taken to heart by anyone seriously considering the purchase of a franchise.

—RAY WILEY, PRESIDENT AND FOUNDER, HOT HEAD BURRITOS AND RAPID FIRED PIZZA

The Franchisee Handbook will take you step-by-step through the process of evaluating franchise opportunities from a more objective viewpoint so you can better evaluate how a particular franchise will work for you and your unique circumstances.

—SCOTT LEHR, EXECUTIVE VICE PRESIDENT OF DEVELOPMENT, MARKETING, AND CONFERENCES FOR THE INTERNATIONAL FRANCHISE ASSOCIATION

The process of investing in a franchise can be difficult to navigate— both for the prospective franchisee and for the franchisor. Mark's book is designed to help you better understand the complexities of this investment that could well alter the course of your life.

—DAVE PAZGAN, CEO, 101 MOBILITY

The Franchisee Handbook provides those who are planning to franchise with a systemized approach to evaluating both themselves and the franchises they are considering. It is an invaluable tool for every would-be franchisee.

—NICK FRIEDMAN, COFOUNDER AND PRESIDENT, COLLEGE H.U.N.K.S. HAULING JUNK

Mark's book will show you how the best franchisors attempt to qualify their franchisees and will provide you with your own framework to evaluate the fit of various franchisors from your perspective. It is an invaluable tool for anyone thinking of buying a franchise.

—SCOT CRAIN, VICE PRESIDENT OF FRANCHISEE RELATIONS, AUNTIE ANNE'S SOFT PRETZELS

As former franchisees, we can attest to the importance of knowing how to look before you leap. *The Franchisee Handbook* provides an invaluable framework for that analysis—both looking at the franchisor and looking at your own capabilities. It is a great first step toward understanding how franchising will work for you.

—CYNTHIA AND STEVE CLARKIN, FORMER FRANCHISEES

With over 3,000 opportunities to choose from, the first-time franchisee may easily find the task of finding that perfect franchise daunting. *The Franchisee Handbook* provides a roadmap to narrowing the field to a manageable number and provides a framework for the kind of diligence and self-examination that will improve anyone's chances of success.

—ALLAN YOUNG, COFOUNDER OF SHELF GENIE

The Franchisee Handbook provides the prospective franchisee with the tools they need to examine the opportunities they are considering and a framework for understanding how they will fit within a particular franchise system. It is a must read for anyone considering a franchise investment.

—PETER ROSS, COFOUNDER AND CEO OF SENIOR HELPERS

The Franchisee Handbook is an essential resource for the would-be franchisee. While I was happy with the franchise I purchased, if I had read this book in advance I might have gone a different direction that would have better suited me personally. I highly recommend this book for anyone who is seriously considering an investment in a franchise.

—BARRY FALCON, FORMER FRANCHISEE AND COFOUNDER OF TWO SUCCESSFUL FRANCHISE COMPANIES

THE
FRANCHISEE
HANDBOOK

EVERYTHING YOU NEED TO KNOW
ABOUT BUYING A FRANCHISE

MARK SIEBERT
CEO OF IFRANCHISE GROUP

Entrepreneur Press®

Entrepreneur Press, Publisher
Cover Design: Andrew Welyczko
Production and Composition: Eliot House Productions

This publication is designed to provide accurate and authoritative information
in regard to the subject matter covered. It is sold with the understanding that
the publisher is not engaged in rendering legal, accounting or other professional
services. If legal advice or other expert assistance is required, the services of a
competent professional person should be sought.

Entrepreneur Press® is a registered trademark of Entrepreneur Media, Inc.

Library of Congress Cataloging-in-Publication Data
Names: Siebert, Mark, 1955- author.
Title: The franchisee handbook: everything you need to know about buying a
    franchise / by Mark Siebert.
Description: Irvine, CA : Entrepreneur Press, [2019]
Identifiers: LCCN 2018038074| ISBN 978-1-59918-639-9 (alk. paper) |
    ISBN 1-59918-639-X (alk. paper)
Subjects: LCSH: Franchises (Retail trade) | Business enterprises—
    Purchasing.
Classification: LCC HF5429.23 .S545 2019 | DDC 658.8/708—dc23
LC record available at https://lccn.loc.gov/2018038074

Printed in the United States of America

23 22 21 20 19   10 9 8 7 6 5 4 3 2 1

CONTENTS

Chapter 2

THE SECRET INGREDIENT: YOU 21

Chapter 3

UNDERSTANDING RISK 33

Chapter 4

NARROWING THE FIELD 51

Appendix C

FOREWORD

BY ROBERT CRESANTI, CFE, PRESIDENT & CEO
INTERNATIONAL FRANCHISE ASSOCIATION

"How do I know if owning a franchise is right for me?" In my role as President and CEO of the International Franchise Association (IFA), I am asked that question all the time. And equally often I am asked, "What is the best franchise to buy?" "How much does it cost to buy a franchise?" and "Is it better to buy a franchise or start my own business?" *The Franchisee Handbook* will help you with these questions and many more you may not even realize you need to ask.

Franchising accounts for nearly 760,000 franchise establishments that support 8.1 million direct jobs, $757 billion of economic output for the U.S. economy and 3 percent of the Gross Domestic Product (GDP).

The International Franchise Association represents franchise companies in over 300 different business format categories. A number of IFA's franchisor members were introduced to our organization by

Mark and Dave's team at iFranchise Group. The iFranchise team has many years of hands-on experience running franchise organizations and meeting with countless people just like you who are thinking of buying their own franchise. That background guides iFranchise Group's and the franchise industry's hallmark principle that franchising is successful when franchisees are successful. Franchisee success is a consistent theme throughout *The Franchisee Handbook*.

Understanding the intricacies of the franchise sales process is at the heart of franchise development. Sometimes both franchisors and prospective franchisees alike need to hear the hard truth about having to turn away a candidate when it is clear the candidate will not be a good fit for the brand and will not be successful. This book will help you appreciate the risks of franchise ownership as well as its many rewards.

The Franchisee Handbook provides a knowledgeable overview of franchising and how it works, and it will help you decide if you are ready to be a franchise owner. It will help you assess the amount of capital you have available, your skills, and your passion for business ownership. Mark takes you through the questions you to need to ask yourself before you can even begin to look at specific franchise concepts and gives you key tools to assess specific concepts. The book will help you understand risk, the kinds of franchise opportunities that are available, and how to discern whether you should move forward. *The Franchisee Handbook* gives you a step-by-step roadmap to the whole process.

As the leader of the world's oldest and largest organization representing the franchise industry, I know people like you. I understand your desire to own something where you can be your own boss, where you can build something with the support of an established brand and industry behind you, and where you can meet your personal and professional goals. I also know that the range of franchise options is exciting and almost limitless, with organizations run by some of the smartest, most innovative business professionals around. I encourage you to explore all that is out there, and I wish you the best.

INTRODUCTION

This is a book about buying a franchise written by someone who has never owned one and likely never will. But make no mistake—I love franchising.

When I took my first job in franchising in 1984, little did I know that it would become a lifelong passion. Franchising has given me the opportunity to work with businesses in almost every imaginable field and in businesses of all shapes and sizes—from single-unit operators to Fortune 500 companies. As one would expect, since a large majority of franchises are food-related, I have had the opportunity to work with dozens and dozens of food-service operators—including companies like Auntie Anne's, Buffalo Wild Wings, Fuzzy's Taco Shop, McAlister's Deli, Newk's Eatery, and many others when they started their franchise journeys. But I have also worked with companies in industries where one might not expect to find franchises. Massage Envy introduced franchising to the market for therapeutic massages.

Sky Zone created an entirely new market for indoor trampoline parks through franchising. Mad Science pioneered and popularized the after-school educational market through franchising. A company called i9 Sports took the organization of youth league sports to the next level using the franchise business model. Senior Helpers was among the first to provide in-home care to seniors through franchising. ShelfGenie and 101 Mobility expanded home improvement and home accessibility services through franchising. Doctors Express (now called American Family Care) pioneered franchising in the health and medical fields. There is no doubt that franchising touches all kinds of industries. And it's a global way of doing business. I have had the opportunity to work with franchise systems in more than two dozen countries. And given the diversity of industries, markets, and organizations with which I have worked, I have had a chance to learn something new each and every day.

As a franchise consultant for more than 30 years, I have had the privilege of working with many of the world's greatest entrepreneurs—a list far, far too long to recount here. I have been honored to know many of the people who have changed the landscape of the world's economy while leaving millionaire franchisees in their wake. And I have had the misfortune of seeing what happens when franchising does not work out for the franchisee.

Despite the occasional failure, I believe franchising is the greatest expansion strategy ever conceived—for both the franchisor and the franchisee. So why haven't I bought one myself? Simply put, I am not cut out for the job. I love what I do far too much to abandon it and follow a system developed by someone else. And, frankly, franchising is not the right path for everyone. In this book, one of the first tasks I will set for you is a brutal self-evaluation. Are you cut out for business ownership? And if you are, are you well-suited to a role in which you will have to adhere to brand standards that are established and enforced by the franchisor?

For those who decide they are well-suited to franchising, choosing a franchise is not an easy task. And I sincerely hope this book will not make it easier. In fact, if this book succeeds in its job, it should make the franchise buying process *more* difficult. It should raise your level of healthy skepticism. It should encourage you to do more homework before making what could be the greatest financial decision of your life. It will help you decide if you are a good fit for franchising, if a particular franchise is a good fit for you, and, ideally, I hope it will help you find the perfect business—or avoid your biggest financial disaster.

Freedom Is in the Eye of the Beholder

The fact is, even if you faithfully follow every step in this book, you cannot take the risk out of the franchise-buying process. For many of you, that may mean jeopardizing your life's savings. It may mean starting down a path that, if you fail, could derail your existing career.

It will certainly mean sacrifice in the short term. People often go into business for themselves for the "freedom" that business ownership provides. And as a business owner myself, I can attest to that freedom. You will have the freedom to work 10 to 12 hours per day, perhaps seven days a week, when you get started. The freedom to watch your key employees leave, probably at the most inopportune times. The freedom to sweat out every payroll. The freedom to wake up in the middle of the night wondering if a 16-year-old kid with an iPhone will post something on the internet so embarrassing that it could cost you your business. And, yes, the freedom to see your child's soccer game in the middle of the week without having to ask your boss for permission—assuming, of course, that you work a few extra hours over the weekend.

But despite all the travails you will face as a business owner, I would recommend it to *almost* everyone. You will be in charge of your own success. You will have the satisfaction that comes only from building something lasting. You will be creating a business that could live beyond you and pass on to your heirs—or that you could one day sell, perhaps achieving generational wealth. You will be able to employ people and watch them flourish, knowing you have helped them buy a house, put food on their table, and educate their kids. And, if you are successful, you will eventually stop sweating the payrolls and have the freedom to enjoy your life in a way that most of those around you cannot.

While the right franchisor will make your journey easier, it will still be up to you to do the hard work. It will be up to you to carry the burden of success. And it will be up to you to shoulder the risk.

Risk vs. Return

In every economics course I have ever taken, the instructor discussed the concept of risk vs. return. A low-risk investment—like a Treasury bill guaranteed by the U.S. government—will provide a lower return. For someone to induce an investor to take a bigger risk, they need to provide a higher return. The greater the perceived risk, the higher the anticipated return.

Never was this maxim in greater need of understanding than in the franchise-buying process. Like any business, franchising carries numerous risks. In many cases, the knowledge gained by the franchisor in developing their prototype operations will help you reduce that risk by allowing you to avoid otherwise costly, and perhaps fatal, mistakes.

While most franchisees are happy with their decision to buy a franchise, unfortunately some are not. Maybe they weren't suited to business ownership. Maybe, like me, they weren't suited for the role of a franchisee. Maybe franchising was right for them, but they chose the wrong industry. Or maybe they purchased a franchise that required more skill or capital than they possessed.

When you consider that buying a franchise not only involves an investment of money but also a commitment of time and effort, choosing the right franchise (or deciding whether to buy a franchise at all) will probably be the biggest financial decision you will make in your life. Not only will it dictate what you will earn and your financial worth, but it may well dictate how you spend your days *for the next decade or more.*

All too many people buy a franchise the way they purchase a car. They may read *Consumer Reports*, absorb the relevant statistics, and talk to friends and salesmen. They look at budgets and gas mileage and safety standards. But in the end, they fall in love with the shiniest car on the lot and rationalize their decision: They need that Porsche because it's easier to park in tight spaces.

How to Use This Book

If you are like most readers, you are about to embark on a journey that may lead to one of the biggest decisions of your life. The goal of this book is to provide you with the tools you need to make that decision. It is not designed to make that decision for you.

This book lays out a series of steps that I think a well-informed prospective franchise buyer should consider in making this decision. I have tried to present these steps in a somewhat logical order, but as you read them, understand that the process of investing in a franchise is a fluid one, and sometimes the steps will occur in a different order. Or, on occasion, you will find there are exceptions to some of these recommendations. For example, one step that is universally recommended in the franchise-buying process is to speak with existing franchisees. But a new franchisor may not yet have any existing franchisees (or the ones they have sold may not yet be open). Likewise, while it is wise to visit franchisor locations, some service businesses may be homebased, denying you that opportunity. While I cannot lay out a definitive path, I hope that by using these steps as a guideline, you can help tilt the risk-reward equation in your favor.

Selecting the right franchise, assuming franchising is right for you at all, isn't just a question of caveat emptor (buyer beware). It's much too complicated for that. And while you should definitely do a level of due diligence on the franchisor, it is perhaps more important that you focus an equal amount of attention on your capabilities to succeed as their franchisee.

When going into business for yourself, you risk your capital, reputation, livelihood, happiness, and a huge investment of your time, in return for the independence and financial rewards that may await you as a business owner. In the end, this book is about assessing these risks and measuring whether they are worth the potential return. You can't avoid risk or guarantee return by reading this book. But I hope it will increase your odds of arriving at the correct conclusion.

One of the goals for this book is to help you avoid failure as you consider the path toward franchise ownership. Here are just a few tips that I'll build upon further throughout the book:

- ✂ As you evaluate franchising, take an honest look at your likely strengths and weaknesses as a potential business owner.
- ✂ Don't underestimate the importance of having a strong support network.
- ✂ Never open a business (franchised or not) unless you have sufficient capital resources.
- ✂ Ensure that any franchise you are strongly considering is a good match with your skill set and personal interests.
- ✂ Be thorough in your due diligence of any franchise system you consider, leveraging as many data points as possible in the evaluation process.

The purpose of this book is *not* to eliminate risk. That is not possible in business. Instead, the purpose of this book is to help you:

- ✂ accurately assess those risks,
- ✂ help you determine if you can afford to take those risks,
- ✂ provide some guidance on how to minimize those risks,
- ✂ and provide you with guidance on how to fairly assess potential returns.

Throughout, I have tried to use clear terms—which is not always easy when writing about a business with very specific terminology and processes. To that end, I will occasionally speak in generalities that are not universally applied within franchising. I have done this to make reading easier, but it occasionally will lead to statements that are not true in all cases.

Some of these shortcuts include the following:

- ✄ In discussing franchise laws, definitions, statistics, and best practices, I have taken the liberty to assume we are talking about the United States, which is the world's largest and most competitive franchise marketplace. For readers outside the U.S., some of what you read may need to be adapted to your particular market. Franchise laws do not exist in some countries, and in others, they are very different from U.S. laws.

- ✄ Royalties are generally collected as a percentage of gross sales (which is how I'll refer to them in this book), but in some systems, they are collected on gross margin. In others, they may be a flat monthly fee. Or they may be offset, in whole or in part, based on revenues that the franchisor is deriving from product sales. Keep in mind you should always check with a prospective franchisor on this point, as it could differ depending on the business.

- ✄ Throughout the book, I may refer to franchisors who provide support in the areas of real estate and site selection. Of course, many franchises are homebased or have very limited real estate needs. Again, this depends largely on the type of franchise you are looking to buy.

- ✄ Other generalities will also have exceptions. And while I have tried to choose my words carefully, discussing every exception would make this book read more like a legal textbook than one focused on making a sound business evaluation.

Ultimately, franchising has many faces—in fact, it has almost as many faces as there are franchisors. I hope that this book will make your franchise selection process easier. But, just like a franchise, this book makes no guarantees. Hopefully, like a good franchisor, it will offer you direction and support. But, as with a franchise, in the end, your success or failure is largely up to you. Good luck on your journey to business ownership.

Chapter 1

THE FRANCHISE MYTH

W e've all heard the stories. How 100 shares of McDonald's initial stock offering back in 1965 would be worth millions today (more precisely, those shares would be worth close to $12 million as of this writing). How no McDonald's franchisee has ever failed (although, like all restaurants, even McDonald's occasionally closes units).

But the stories that really get our hearts pumping are the ones where a friend of a friend became a multimillionaire by buying the right franchise at the right time. Today they own a dozen locations (along with two houses, three cars, a boat, and a plane). And those stories sound all the more intriguing when we hear that the franchisee was just a regular person. Not some rocket scientist who was always destined for success. Not some rich kid who parlayed Daddy's small fortune into a bigger fortune of their own. Just a person with a dream, a little money, and a lot of courage.

We could have done that, too—if only . . .

We tend to believe the myth, but what is the reality? What is this magic system, and just how magic is it anyway?

Busting the Franchise Myth

Franchising is, without a doubt, one of the most powerful business expansion strategies in the world today. It has helped some of the world's most iconic brands expand far faster than they could have ever dreamed of growing organically. But how did it go mainstream? The answer lies in franchising's fraught beginnings.

Early franchisors, like A&W Restaurants, Howard Johnson's, Midas, McDonald's, Century 21, and others, got their start before today's franchise regulations. Back in those days, franchising was a loosely defined concept, but the early successes of these companies popularized franchising as never before.

By the early 1960s, hundreds of new franchisors were entering the market. Still, franchising was only a small part of the U.S. economy. Unfortunately, along with the legitimate businesses that were getting into franchising, there were some that ended up as well-publicized failures—and in some cases, outright fraud. For example:

✂ In the wake of Kentucky Fried Chicken's success, John Jay Hooker—a politician with no restaurant experience—created and quickly franchised a concept called Minnie Pearl's Chicken. When the company began franchising in 1967, it had yet to open its first location. But based on the celebrity endorsement of the country comedian, Hooker sold 300 franchises by early 1968 and went public only months later with just a handful of restaurants open. By 1970, Minnie Pearl's had opened some 250 locations—and had closed more than half of them! Most of the remaining restaurants were losing money. The SEC later launched an investigation into the company's accounting practices—eventually forcing the company to liquidate under the pressure of shareholder lawsuits.

✄ Comedian Jerry Lewis also got in on the act when he partnered with Network Cinema Corporation in 1969 to launch
Jerry Lewis Cinemas as a franchise. Like Minnie Pearl's,
Jerry Lewis Cinemas featured a high-profile endorser and a
business model that did not work. Full-page ads in *Variety*
magazine urged, "Join Jerry Lewis in the most successful
money making segment of the entertainment industry."
By the mid-1970s, the chain had as many as 200 locations
before the business collapsed under the weight of its failed
franchisees.

✄ Not to be outdone, TV host and comedian Johnny Carson
partnered with the Swanson family to launch a hamburger
and fried chicken franchise called "Here's Johnny's" in 1969.
Again, hundreds of franchises were sold, most closed quickly,
and the company declared bankruptcy ten years later.

Of course, this wasn't just some evil cabal of comedians. There
were many other early franchisors, some with good intentions
and some without, that made headlines when their get-rich-quick
schemes and high-pressure sales tactics resulted in hundreds of
failed franchisees. And while the families who invested in franchises
like McDonald's were living the American Dream, others were living
the American nightmare.

It was against this backdrop that, in 1972, the first of the state
franchise laws was passed in California. Essentially, the law required
franchisors to make presale disclosures to prospective franchisees
to allow them to make an "informed decision" on their investment.
Other states followed California's lead, and in 1979, Congress passed
FTC Rule 436, commonly called the Franchise Rule. According to this
law, which was updated in 2007, prospective franchisees must receive
a prescribed disclosure document (called a Franchise Disclosure
Document, or FDD) regarding the franchisor and the contents of their
contract prior to exercising the franchise agreement. (We will go into
much greater detail on the FDD in Chapter 5, but for now, you should
know that it is designed to protect potential franchise buyers by

giving them the information they need to make an informed decision on the purchase of a franchise.)

In creating this rule, lawmakers had to define just what a "franchise" was, so they could determine whether or not the rule applied to a specific business. In layman's terms, FTC Rule 436 defines a business as a franchise if it meets **all three** of the following criteria:

1. It allows the franchisee to use its name or trademark in association with a business.
2. It provides significant operating assistance or exercises significant control over the franchisee (providing operations manuals, training, a protected territory, and many, other things can trigger this provision of the definition).
3. It collects a fee (which can be an upfront franchise fee, a royalty, a product markup beyond the wholesale price, or any of a number of other ways franchisors make money off franchisees).

While some states that have separate regulations governing franchise sales have their own definitions of what constitutes a franchise (and when a franchisor must register their franchise to sell in that state), for our purposes, it is easiest to think of a franchise as a company that offers you the right to operate using their name and business system in return for a fee. While some early franchisors viewed the model as a get-rich-quick scheme, their mistakes helped create laws that protect us today.

No Longer a Punchline

While the early days of franchising saw both visionary entrepreneurs and slick salespeople armed with poor business models, franchising today has evolved into one of the most dominant methods of business expansion and ownership in the U.S.

As more and more businesses adopted franchising as a way to expand, and more franchisees gained experience in their roles, education and best practices specific to franchising began to develop and create the culture of franchising in this country. Federal and state laws were established to better define and regulate franchise relationships. Franchisors learned the importance of systems that were mutually beneficial to the franchisor and their franchisees. In 1960, the International Franchise Association (IFA) was founded to promote franchising. Today, the IFA is a powerful force representing the interests of both franchisors and franchisees.

Many years ago, the U.S. Department of Commerce characterized franchising as "the wave of the future"—and in the U.S., that wave has been landing for the past seven decades. The result of this prolonged trend is the largest franchise economy in the world.

According to the "Franchise Business Economic Outlook for 2018" report prepared by IHS Markit Economics for the IFA Franchise Education and Research Foundation, there are some 759,000 franchise businesses (i.e., individual franchise locations) in the U.S. Altogether, they directly employ more than 8 million people and generate more than $750 billion in economic output. Today's franchisees are more sophisticated and knowledgeable about franchising than ever before. More of them own multiple locations, and are even franchisees of multiple franchise systems. The advancement and integration of technology within franchising has also contributed a great deal to the success of franchising as a business model. Better technology has facilitated the development of operations training, data accumulation, benchmarking of financial data, and the dissemination of best practices within franchise systems.

That said, it is easy to understand why the growth of franchising isn't front-page news. After all, the jobs are added a few at a time, as opposed to the Fortune 500 companies that might open a factory employing hundreds or even thousands of people—or lay off 1,000 or more workers at a time. Perhaps the more important question, though, is why franchising continues to record such consistent growth even when the rest of the economy is faltering. To find out, let's take a quick look at how it works.

How Does It Work?

Franchising has a basic formula. Usually, after selecting the franchise you want to purchase and going through the required presale disclosures (more on that in Chapter 5), you will be asked to sign a lengthy contract (called a franchise agreement) that will limit how you do business. When you sign, you will pay an initial franchise fee, which typically ranges between $25,000 and $50,000, for the right to enter this business relationship (and for the franchisor's help in the process of starting up your business). Occasionally that initial fee might be nonexistent, while in other instances it can be $150,000 or even higher.

As the franchisee, you will be responsible for all startup costs associated with opening your new business. For a site-specific business, you will probably (although not always) be required to find your own site and negotiate your own lease, according to parameters provided by the franchisor. You will be responsible for the costs of land, building, furniture, fixtures, leasehold improvements, equipment, and the initial working capital required to start the business and get it to and beyond break-even. You will have all the responsibility of hiring, training, supervising, and firing your employees. In a nutshell, you will have full financial and operational responsibility for the franchise business, just as you would with any other business.

Here is where it differs: In addition to paying the upfront fees, you will generally be required to pay a royalty ranging from 4 percent to 8 percent of gross revenue—although I have seen royalties that are nonexistent (wrapped into product sales), and I have seen royalties as high as 15 percent. In a number of franchises, the franchisee will be expected to purchase a specified amount of their initial and ongoing inventory from the franchisor or a designated affiliate company. The nature and amount of these royalties and product markups will vary, as you will see in Chapter 5.

In return, the franchisor will allow you to use its name (although you will have no rights to the name or its associated goodwill). The franchisor will train you on how to run the business, and you must pass the initial training before finalizing the grant of your franchise. Generally, the franchisor will also:

- ✄ provide you with startup assistance, perhaps including help with site selection and lease negotiation;
- ✄ work with you and your team at your location during any grand opening;
- ✄ give you ongoing support in running your business, often in the form of purchasing power, advertising and marketing development, product development, ongoing concept refinement, and field consulting.

Since franchisees are burdened with additional startup costs and ongoing fees, including royalties, it is only fair to ask why this model works as well as it does.

Why Does Franchising Work?

One of the major reasons for the success of franchise systems stems from the nature of franchising itself. As a potential buyer, it is important to understand that franchising is not cutting-edge technology. It is not a strategy to fix a business that is broken. It is a means of expanding a business *that is already highly successful.*

Franchises succeed where new businesses fail for a number of reasons, the most important of which is that they are using proven business systems to market proven products and/or services. When I do seminars for entrepreneurs around the country, I often ask them to imagine that every store they own burned to the ground. I then ask what would happen if they were to take their insurance money and move to an entirely new city to start all over again. Virtually all the entrepreneurs I meet say without hesitation that they would succeed all over again. If I ask them what would happen if an otherwise sharp businessperson with no knowledge of their business but an equal amount of capital were to try to duplicate their success in a new market, they inevitably feel the newcomer would fail.

I then ask them to estimate how a franchisee of their business would perform, assuming they were adequately capitalized and followed the franchisor's system to the letter. And almost all of them agree that the hypothetical performance of their franchisees would exceed their own experience when they first started.

Perhaps this is just the hubris of the type of entrepreneurs who are drawn to franchising, but I personally believe it to be true. They have it figured out. They know where the land mines are buried and how to build their business quickly. While I can only rely on anecdotal evidence to back this claim, this tends to be the case in real life as well. And it is that system of operations that you are investing in when you purchase a franchise.

How Franchising Benefits Franchisees

The trust you put into a franchisor is your buy-in. That trust exists because the first element in almost every successful franchise is a proven prototype. Franchisors have made many of the mistakes and subsequent course corrections that will allow you to avoid costly errors during the crucial startup phase. Franchises are systems that have been tested and refined and tested again. And gaining access to that system gives you, as a franchisee, the ability to start faster, reduce your initial investment, and avoid mistakes.

Avoiding mistakes can start before you have even opened your doors for business. As an example, for site-specific businesses, nowhere are these mistakes more impactful than in the area of site selection and lease negotiation. In retail or restaurant operations, assistance with site location and lease negotiation can mean the difference between success and failure. Pick the wrong site or sign a bad lease, and you may have a long-term problem for which no solution exists.

Before you open your doors for business, most franchisors will provide initial training on every aspect of the business—from finding a site to build-out to hiring and training your team to serving your customers to managing your business. And for most franchisors, that training is just the start. Franchisors generally provide detailed operations manuals that explain how to deal with most situations that are likely to arise in your day-to-day operations. Many provide significant ongoing training.

Other startup support can be similarly valuable. Knowing what inventory to stock can make a huge difference in cash flow during the critical early months. Knowing what equipment to purchase, and at what price and terms, can have an enormous impact on efficiency and profitability. The franchisor can help franchisees avoid mistakes in dozens of areas: the right mix of products or services, appropriate pricing, effective advertising media selection, compelling messaging, vendor selection and negotiation, and labor management are some of the more important areas where the franchisor can add value. Moreover, the franchisor will generally provide ongoing support—in the form of phone support and a field representative who will visit periodically—as both a business coach and to ensure you and the other franchisees in the system are living up to the brand standards that made the concept successful in the first place.

There are other advantages to purchasing a franchise, as well.

Goodwill

Regardless of whether the franchisor has one unit or 10,000, it is certain to have more name recognition than you would have as a startup business. And if that name recognition carries with it some goodwill at the consumer level, you as a franchisee will benefit from it.

This is especially true if you are buying a service-based franchise. As an unaffiliated startup business, your sales pitch to new customers might be, "I am just starting this business and may have no experience, but I will work hard on your behalf." As a franchisee, it becomes, "We have been in this business for XX years and have serviced accounts including X, Y, and Z, who would be happy to provide stellar references. We are now expanding into your city, and I was wondering if I could speak to you about getting your business."

Cost Benefits

Another advantage to buying a franchise is somewhat counterintuitive: Franchises can be less expensive to open than independent businesses. It's hard to believe—as a franchisee, you have to pay a franchise fee of $25,000 to $50,000 or more. But it is true. Why?

As a franchisee, you'll know precisely what inventory to buy and what equipment to lease. And you'll probably get better prices due to the franchisor's ability to purchase in volume and pricing arrangements with suppliers. You'll learn how to promote your business without wasting your time and money on advertising that doesn't work. You will be able to control your startup costs and avoid mistakes that could cost tens of thousands of dollars. You'll benefit from the franchisor's experience in dozens of ways that will help you reduce expenses while increasing your revenues.

Additionally, the franchisor has already assumed many expenses that you as a franchisee will not have to undertake, including registering its trademark, designing a logo, developing a brand website and consumer advertising materials, creating proprietary recipes (if it's a food-based business), developing basic merchandising schemes, and establishing supply chain relationships and negotiated discounts.

Bottom line: In many franchise businesses, you'll probably be cash flow positive sooner than your nonfranchise counterpart, despite paying a franchise fee. This is especially likely if you're a first-time business owner. So while your startup costs may be increased by the franchise fee, they will often be much lower overall.

Similarly, while your operation will be burdened with having to pay the franchisor an ongoing royalty, you will gain the support, established systems, and brand recognition provided by the franchisor. Many franchisors will have developed strong, proven marketing campaigns that you can use to leverage their already established brand. They may have better buying power, again saving you substantial expenses. And for some franchisors, the ability to secure national accounts on your behalf may provide additional benefits.

Staying Power

Finally, when it comes time for you to sell your business, a franchise may command a higher price. This advantage is easy to understand. If you were thinking of purchasing a business and had your choice between a McDonald's and Joe's Burgers, if all other things (like profitability) were equal, which would you rather purchase?

Let's think about it. While buying a McDonald's doesn't guarantee that you would earn money, it's likely the handoff to a new owner will be easy. That's because McDonald's has the operational manuals and expertise to help you ensure a smooth transition. Moreover, McDonald's patrons know what to expect out of any McDonald's restaurant, because McDonald's spends a great deal of time and effort ensuring this consistency. With Joe's Burgers, the minute Joe walks out the door, half his customers might follow him—and who is going to help in the transition process? Who will ensure quality control?

Most people would certainly prefer to buy the McDonald's, and thus its owner could command a higher selling price.

At the same time, ask yourself: Which of these units has the greatest potential? Joe's Burgers does, of course. Because you could turn Joe's Burgers into a chain—perhaps even a franchise chain—yourself, thus reaping far greater rewards.

While the brand is part of it, your real value proposition lies in the quality of the system and the amount of support provided by the franchisor. Ultimately, the secret to the success of most franchisors is that they make a lot of money for their franchisees. Franchisors whose franchisees become millionaires have no problems finding more franchisees.

When Does It Not Work?

Unfortunately, franchisors whose franchisees are destined to struggle may also attract their fair share of buyers—especially when the franchise concept is shiny and new (and there are no failed franchisees yet to spread the word).

Sometimes, the reason a franchise fails can be traced to a poor concept. The franchisor simply had not adequately refined the business model before taking the franchise to market.

Sometimes it can be attributed to lack of franchisor support. A franchisor may have a great concept but lack the ability to help their franchisees succeed. Perhaps they didn't have the right people. Perhaps their growth outstripped their ability to support their franchisees.

And sometimes, the problem can be traced to the individual franchisees they recruited. They weren't smart enough, they didn't work hard enough, they didn't have enough capital or the right skill set. Or perhaps it was just bad luck: Death, divorce, illness, unforeseen financial circumstances, or any number of other events can turn success into failure.

The best franchisors have systems in place to try to ensure that the franchisees they recruit have a strong chance of success. The best franchisors will display a high degree of integrity when it comes to franchisee selection. Ultimately, while a franchise salesperson's goal is to earn commissions, a franchisor's goal is to successfully grow their system, and that won't happen if their franchisees fail.

Unfortunately, there is no test that can consistently predict success or failure. Even the best businesses sometimes slip up, and the best systems for screening prospective franchisees will occasionally fail.

So some of the burden of franchisee selection—and some of the fault for failure—must be borne by the franchisee. If you are serious about buying a franchise, you need to take responsibility for making the right choice.

What's in It for the Franchisor?

The purpose of this book, of course, is to provide the reader with a framework for making one of the biggest decisions of their life. As part of that process, I think it is important to understand the motives of the folks on the other side of the table. Why have they chosen to franchise? And what are the implications for you?

There are a variety of reasons that companies choose to franchise; some of them are obvious, while others may be somewhat subtler. The primary reason companies decide to franchise, and probably the most important to you, is a lack of capital.

In franchising, the franchisor generates less revenue per unit (since it is only earning royalties and perhaps product sales or lease revenue) than it would if it owned that operation outright. Assuming that a corporate location is profitable, the franchisor is also likely to achieve lower profits (in terms of total dollars) on a per-unit basis as well. But in terms of return on invested capital (ROIC), a company will achieve significantly higher leverage through franchising, and thus generally a much higher ROIC.

For these companies, franchising is a very attractive alternative because it allows them to expand using OPM—other people's money.

Another reason for franchising involves the rate at which a company can hope to expand. Even companies with plenty of capital find they can expand much more quickly by franchising.

In order for a company to open a single unit, it must look at dozens of sites, determine the best choice, negotiate the lease, arrange for an architect to design the interior, hire a contractor for the build-out, negotiate equipment leases, purchase initial inventory, hire and train managers and staff, and prepare for the grand opening. With a franchise program, a company can depend on its franchisees for most of this—it merely provides the training in how to execute each of these steps.

Franchising also allows franchisors to eliminate their responsibility for the daily operations of their business, thus allowing them to grow using a leaner management structure. Franchisors do not need big Personnel Departments to screen, hire, fire, and motivate employees. Franchisors do not need the staff of bookkeepers and payroll staff necessary to pay hundreds of employees. Franchisors simply delegate this responsibility to their franchisees.

A third major reason for franchising is its ability to motivate the "manager" at the unit level. Over the years, we have found that franchisees will often outperform company-owned units, both in terms of revenues and expense management. One company I worked with early in my career, Sterling Optical, sold about 60 existing units as franchises and saw the average store sales at those units jump through the roof.

Some franchisors, large manufacturers in particular, choose to franchise because they want to sell product, and they want to lock in their channel of distribution. Franchising, with its emphasis on quality control, allows them to do just that.

In a nutshell, those are the biggest reasons that companies franchise. Money. Time. People. Economies of scale. Risk reduction. Locking in a channel of distribution.

Money

Why are those considerations important for you as a buyer? First, you need to be aware that your franchisor may not be well-capitalized—potentially limiting their ability to provide you with support. Early stage franchisors often start franchising with very limited resources. In many cases, the principals of neophyte franchisors must wear multiple hats: business owner, innovator, franchise marketer, franchise salesperson, franchise trainer, franchise real estate manager, grand opening coordinator, and field support consultant. And it is likely they will be better at some roles than others.

To best leverage their time, many of these newer franchisors may outsource a number of these jobs to focus on their core competencies. Outsourcing marketing, sales, real estate selection, and construction assistance is now fairly commonplace in franchising. But franchisors who do not avail themselves of these services may find themselves stretched thin if they grow too fast.

Larger franchise companies, on the other hand, will have more financial and human resources to allocate to you. They may have specialists in each of these areas. And the largest franchisors will have teams devoted to each.

This, of course, does not mean you should only consider established franchisors in your selection process. When John Leonesio started Massage Envy, he did not have teams of people to support his franchisees. But the concept was extremely well-positioned and differentiated, and many of the franchisees who jumped in early are multimillionaires today.

A franchisor's capitalization—and how they choose to grow their franchise—is simply one risk factor you need to consider in making your decision.

Time

Second, you need to be aware that your franchisor will likely ask you to do much of the heavy lifting when it comes to opening and operating your business. If you believe the franchisor will do everything for you, you will probably be sadly mistaken. Even in the largest franchise organizations, you will be responsible for most of the work required to get started.

Remember that a franchise relationship is very different from an employer-employee relationship. As a franchisee, you are an independent business owner. In virtually every franchise, you will make the final decision on where to locate the business. You will almost always be responsible for deciding which contractors to use in the construction and build-out of your operation. You will make all decisions relative to financing the business and hiring your employees. You will typically be responsible for training them, scheduling them, and supervising their work. You will generally make most decisions regarding pricing your goods and services. And ultimately, you will typically make all decisions about day-to-day unit operations. Your decisions will determine the success or failure of your business.

People

Finally, franchisors want to leverage off of the efforts of highly motivated owner-operators like you—who have invested their life's savings in the business. Like the old joke about the bacon and egg breakfast, the chicken is involved and the pig (or in this case, the franchisee) is, much to the delight of the franchisor, committed. The franchisor also benefits from the fact that, unlike a manager that may leave at the drop of a hat, you will be with the franchised business for the long term, accumulating knowledge and experience along the route.

But from the buyer's point of view, you need to understand that you are contractually obligated to a long-term relationship with your franchisor—so you need to be certain that you choose correctly. It is highly unlikely that your franchise comes with a money-back guarantee. Nor will it come with a "walk-away" clause. In many cases, you may be entering an agreement in which you have an ongoing obligation to operate the franchise and pay royalties to the franchisor (and you may be signing a long-term property lease or equipment leases with similar provisions). Often you will need to sign a personal guarantee. And while most franchise agreements have clauses that allow you to sell your franchise, even that right is restricted. Of course, there may not be much of a market for a failing franchise even if the franchisor supports your resale.

Other Benefits

Aside from the primary benefits of time, people, and money, companies are also motivated to franchise by many other factors. For one thing, because a franchisor grows using other people's money, they risk very little of their own capital (relatively speaking) on their growth. When the franchisee opens a market, the franchisor generally buys no vehicles or equipment, does not pay for any buildout, and signs no leases. They do not employ people at the unit level. So all of that risk is left to you, the franchisee (ideally along with a significant portion of the return on that investment).

Likewise, another big motivator for new franchisors are the economies of scale that can be harvested as their network grows. These economies of scale can come in the form of the increased buying power of a larger network of locations. They can come in the form of increased advertising strength, which will benefit both franchised stores and their existing company locations. And they may come in the form of a newfound ability to open up national accounts based on the increased or deeper geographical coverage that a larger network can bring.

So while the best franchisors will be just as cautious in helping their franchisees expand as they would if they were investing their own money, some franchisors may have a different perspective on what is an acceptable level of risk when they are using your dollars. And likewise, a franchisor's need to open more locations or in new markets may motivate them to take on franchisees that might not be an ideal fit—even if they are not consciously lowering their standards. So it is up to you to be sure that you understand the franchisor's motives and mindset when sorting through what you hear about any particular franchise opportunity.

Don't Believe the Statistics

In franchising, you will occasionally hear folks tout industry success rates. One figure that was bandied about for years was the assertion that between 4 percent and 5 percent of franchise businesses close in any given year. They would then compare that failure rate with the much higher failure rate of new businesses in the hope of getting prospective franchisees to conclude that franchising was far safer.

The only problem is that the failure rate of franchises was simply made up. In the U.S., there is no federal requirement to register a franchise, and about half the states have no requirements to register or file disclosure documents either. For that reason alone, it is impossible to compile a comprehensive list of franchisors—let alone how many of their franchisees fail in any given year.

Moreover, the information reported in these disclosure documents does not allow for the kind of analysis that will accurately count business failures. For example, the FDD tracks something called a "transfer rate," which looks at when a franchise is sold to another franchisee. If someone invests $250,000 in opening a location, earns $100,000 a year, and then sells the business five years later for $500,000, that is called a transfer. Likewise, someone could invest the same $250,000, lose money every year (only keeping it open by working for free), and sell the business at a huge loss—and that would also count as a transfer. One success story. One failure. Same statistic.

But perhaps most important from your standpoint, how the franchise "industry" does as a whole has *absolutely nothing* to do with how a particular franchise concept will perform. Franchising, in fact, is not an industry. It is a channel of distribution. As such, talking about the success of franchising is no more relevant than talking about the success rate of joint ventures.

It is also important to note that even if you look at failure rates on a franchisor-by-franchisor basis, you still may not have an adequate measure of risk. For example, a younger franchisor that has sold 20 franchises in its first three years may have had zero failures, transfers, and nonrenewals. At the same time, a ten-year-old franchise company with 50 units might have had five closures. So which has the higher risk? Unfortunately, it may be impossible to say. Some of the older franchisor's closures might have been due to the death of a franchisee or other factors beyond the franchisor's control. And the younger franchisor may have 20 failing franchisees who simply have not yet run out of time and money.

While certain statistics, if relevant, can aid you in assessing risk, there is no single statistic that, in and of itself, is a reliable indicator.

Let Risk vs. Reward Be Your Guide

In economics, one of the underlying principles is that of risk vs. reward. In essence, it states that the greater the risk, the greater the perceived reward must be to motivate someone to take that risk.

You probably know this instinctively. If we leave our money in the bank, up to $250,000 is insured by the Federal Deposit Insurance Company, making it nearly risk free. But in today's marketplace, it will yield a return well under 1 percent. On the other hand, if you invest that money in a franchise, your risk increases significantly. So you will want to receive more money for your investment.

To be clear: There is nothing wrong with risk. I expect some of the readers of this book will be very risk averse. Others will be willing to take larger risks in an effort to reap larger rewards. But regardless of your degree of risk tolerance, it is vitally important to come to a realistic appraisal of risk vs. returns before investing in a franchise.

With this in mind, I have developed a process you can follow in making your investment decision to help you assess and measure risk vs. return.

THE BOTTOM LINE: SUCCESS IN BUSINESS IS *NOT* A MATTER OF LUCK

As you prepare yourself for business ownership, you should understand that some businesses will fail simply because of bad luck or poor timing—and sometimes there is nothing you can do about it. Perhaps there is an earthquake, a flood, or an unforeseen problem with the supply chain. Perhaps there was an unforeseeable change in demand, the entry of new competitors into the marketplace, or the development of a new and improved technology. Perhaps it was as simple as the road in front of your shop closing, a dip in the economy, or bad PR caused by an event beyond your control. And while a prudent businessperson will plan for most contingencies, you simply cannot take all the risk out of a business venture.

But while businesses sometimes fail due to bad luck, the converse is almost never true: They rarely succeed because of good luck. That may be enough for a flash-in-the-pan business—like the guy with a snowplow on the front of his truck when a big storm hits—but it won't sustain a company in the long run.

The entrepreneurs in my audiences know what they need to do to run a successful business. They know how to buy the right amount of the right inventory, find a good site and negotiate a favorable lease, buy the right equipment at the right price and on the right terms, institute quality control systems, measure the key performance indicators that will impact their business and understand what they mean, and respond to inevitable problems as they are identified.

There are a thousand little things that will influence your success in business, and for any of us to succeed, we need to do most of them right. The best entrepreneurs know (or find out) how to do that and have developed systems to replicate their success.

This is the knowledge that you, as a prospective franchisee, are thinking about purchasing. It's more than the "secret sauce" that goes on the bun, it's the basics of how to run the business. It's how to open the doors in the morning and close them in the evening—and everything in between.

All these advantages really amount to this: As a franchisee, you will trade two things to get two things. You give up a degree of independence and agree to pay certain fees in return for a reduced risk of failure and the advantages and support that are generally associated with bigger, more sophisticated companies.

The real question you must answer is whether this trade-off is worth it for you.

Chapter 2

THE SECRET INGREDIENT: YOU

We talked in Chapter 1 about the franchisor's "secret sauce"— the intellectual property they have developed that will allow you to succeed. The value proposition offered by every franchisor should always focus on providing you with the knowledge and tools that will make you successful.

In examining any franchise opportunity, you can count on very few things being similar. Franchising is as diverse as small business itself. The franchises you encounter will have different products and services, offer different fees and startup investments, and address different markets using different advertising and messaging.

But perhaps most important from a buyer's perspective, they will all require different skills to succeed. Some franchises will work best if you are a tenacious salesperson. Others may require you to be adept at management. Still others may require particular technical skills or industry expertise.

The one thing every franchise you will consider will have in common—and the one thing that will most influence the success or failure of that franchise—is *you.*

So before you address the question of what business you should be in, you should start with some basic introspection. Because while the franchisor may have the secret sauce to make a business operate well, you are the secret ingredient to making it succeed.

Know Thyself!

Before you decide to buy a franchise, you must first decide whether you are ready for business ownership at all. That might sound like an easy question to my readers. Of course you are ready. But think again. Business ownership has been so extolled in America that you likely do not have a clear picture of what it is all about unless you have already owned a business in the past.

Business ownership means you will be your own boss. And that sounds fun and exciting—until you find out that you are also in charge of cleaning the toilets. You will no longer have an assistant to bring you a cup of coffee in the morning. When someone calls in sick at 5 a.m., you need to get out of bed and go to work in their place. You will also have to fire that employee who isn't quite cutting it—even if it's your best friend.

Business ownership means independence, but it also means dependence. Your business will depend on you to be there, and you'll never be completely free of it. For the first couple of years, you may work 60 or 70 hours a week—or more! No paid vacations. No putting it all behind you when you go home to dinner—you'll eat, drink, and sleep your business. To paraphrase Shakespeare, the world is your office. And when you finally do take that first well-deserved vacation, you'll worry about how things are going without you. You'll give your employees your phone number "just in case something happens," and you'll call in twice a day anyway.

In time, as you get your business established, you'll be able to take an afternoon off to watch your child's baseball game. But at the beginning it will mean working nights and weekends—and perhaps some holidays.

Business ownership means controlling your own destiny. It also means increased responsibility. Are you going to make payroll this week? Do you tell the single mother of two working for you that you've funded advertising before payroll when it's the week before Christmas? Or do you dip into your kid's college fund to cover it?

According to Investopedia (https://www.investopedia.com/), business ownership is the single most well-traveled route to financial independence. It has been reported that nearly half of the world's millionaires accumulated their money through business ownership. It can also be a road to financial ruin. New businesses often fail, and franchise businesses are not immune. Business ownership means you could lose *everything*: your car repossessed, your house foreclosed, your family on the street.

Business ownership means prestige, but it also means your banker could turn down your home loan application because you have not been in business long enough.

Ask yourself if you have the personality of a successful business owner. I have found that successful business owners are generally:

- ✂ goal oriented,
- ✂ extremely focused,
- ✂ high energy,
- ✂ self-starters,
- ✂ conscious of details,
- ✂ adept at multitasking,
- ✂ capable of delegation,
- ✂ patient,
- ✂ extremely optimistic, and
- ✂ strong (and sometimes even inspirational) leaders.

Does that list sound like you?

As a business owner, you will need to motivate yourself. It is all too easy to sleep in on Saturday after a long week, but as a startup business owner, you may not have that luxury. And there will be no one else there to get you going in the morning.

Starting a business invariably means setbacks. When that happens, will you have the resilience to persevere? Or will you let these difficulties weigh you down?

Starting a business also means uncertainty. You will wonder on more than one occasion if you made the right decision. You will worry about whether you will make your next payroll and about what will happen if a key employee leaves. That is part of the job. If these concerns will keep you up night after night, perhaps business ownership is not for you.

Before deciding to go into business for yourself, consider your goals and objectives. Examine your tolerance for risk—are you willing to risk your capital and perhaps work 60 or 70 hours a week to achieve those goals?

Be sure you have a support system in place to help you through the tough times. Discuss your goals with your spouse or partner, because he or she will share the risks and the worry—and may end up helping with some of the financial burden. Then decide for yourself if business ownership is for you.

Are You an Entrepreneur?

A completely separate question is whether you are an entrepreneur. Often, when we think about entrepreneurship, we do so in positively charged terms. We like to think of ourselves as bold, decisive, independent leaders. But by definition, most of us cannot be leaders. There can only be so many.

While we like being associated with the positive elements of entrepreneurship, we must also recognize that there are entrepreneurial traits that can be problematic in a franchise setting.

It is often said that the motto of the true entrepreneur is "Ready, Fire, Aim."

The following definition of an entrepreneur pops up in various places on the internet:

en·tre·pre·neur

,äntrəprænər/

noun

1. a person who organizes and operates a business or businesses, taking on greater than normal financial risks in order to do so.

But my personal definition of an entrepreneur is "someone who never saw a rule that they did not want to break."

Because a franchisee is an independent business owner, of course, they will need to be an entrepreneur at some level. They need to think on their feet and make day-to-day decisions for their business. They need to take the risks and work the long hours that are typical of traditional entrepreneurs.

Over the years, I have identified a number of characteristics of entrepreneurs that tend to define the type. While this list does not necessarily apply to every single entrepreneur, my personal experience has shown that many entrepreneurs tend to:

- ✄ start their first business by the age of 25,
- ✄ move frequently from job to job,
- ✄ be willing to gamble everything on their personal performance,
- ✄ be very optimistic, even in the face of dire odds,
- ✄ be sales and marketing oriented,
- ✄ be visionary in their management approach, but not necessarily good day-to-day managers,
- ✄ be extremely driven (often sacrificing important aspects of their personal lives for their businesses),
- ✄ see the world in terms of great opportunities, and
- ✄ be rule breakers in every sense of the word.

Do these criteria remind you of yourself? Or are you closer to the dictionary definition of an entrepreneur? If they do, you may want to consider whether you can live by someone else's rules.

Rule Breakers Make Lousy Franchisees

When most people envision the characteristics of a successful franchisee, their first thought is that the candidate should have the entrepreneurial spirit. And that is certainly true. But if you look at the character traits above, it's clear that what sets some entrepreneurs apart from the crowd is their disdain for rules.

Unfortunately, when considering a franchise, this trait will only cause you and your franchisor grief.

Ask yourself why, when you're in a distant city looking for a quick bite, you pull into a McDonald's (as a majority of all Americans did last year) instead of Joe's Burgers. Is it because McDonald's serves the best burger on the planet? Hardly—in all the national taste tests I've seen over the years, I've never seen McDonald's rank higher than third.

The reason we pull into McDonald's is because we know *exactly* what to expect. We know a Big Mac will have two all-beef patties, special sauce, lettuce, cheese, pickles, and onion on a sesame seed bun. We know we will be served quickly, and the food will have a consistent taste and quality from visit to visit. Why? Because McDonald's vigilantly ensures that *all* its franchisees meet those exacting brand standards.

If we went to a McDonald's in Tennessee and found they had substituted catfish for the usual pollock in their Filet-O-Fish or to a McDonald's in Chicago and found hot dogs instead of hamburgers, we wouldn't know what to expect—and maybe then we would try Joe's Burgers.

Entrepreneurs (in the traditional sense) and franchisees just don't mix. Entrepreneurs are always trying to "fix" the system, looking to disrupt it, to make a better mousetrap. But the underlying principle of franchising is that the mousetrap is *already* perfect—or at least working well enough to duplicate the business with consistent success. And while all businesses evolve, it is up to the franchisor to lead the charge on this evolution—with franchisees relegated to a role of making suggestions at best. Because ultimately, it is the franchisor's responsibility to continue to adapt the brand and dictate brand standards.

My advice to franchisors, most of whom are entrepreneurs in the first place, is that if someone who reminds them of themselves is interested in buying their franchise, they should run for cover and never look back. Entrepreneurial franchisees can ruin a system faster than they can build it.

This is not to say that franchisees should not be allowed input into the system. Most good franchisors solicit franchisee opinions, as they recognize that franchisees are often closer to the consumer than they are. Many of McDonald's most successful products (including the Big Mac and the Egg McMuffin) have come from franchisees, but they were required to go through channels before the products were even tested! It is said that Ray Kroc, the man who made McDonald's what it is today, once bet McDonald's franchisee Lou Groen that Kroc's Hula Burger—grilled pineapple with cheese on a bun—would outsell the Filet-O-Fish that Groen had created to help attract his Catholic customers (who abstained from eating meat on Fridays at the time). He was wrong—and thousands of Filet-O-Fish sandwiches sold year-round (but especially during Lent) proved the point.

But McDonald's franchisees generally do not have the latitude to experiment with the menu. And you will not be able to experiment with the products and services associated with the franchise you purchase, either.

If you have a true entrepreneurial mindset and you purchase a franchise, you will find yourself in one of three situations:

1. You will constantly battle the franchisor over how you run your business, and, depending on how stubborn you are, you may end up either terminated, nonrenewed, or in court.
2. You will follow the system as dictated, but will bemoan the day you bought the franchise, going through the motions every day believing you could be doing better if you weren't trapped in this relationship.

3. Your franchisor will not enforce standards of quality and consistency on you or your fellow franchisees, and experimenting
   entrepreneurs will cause overall system performance to suffer.

Ask yourself if you can follow the rules and standards established
by the franchisor—even if you disagree with them. Can you trust
someone else to set the standards for a brand in which you will
invest?

There is a big difference between being a true entrepreneur and
having an entrepreneurial spirit. An entrepreneurial spirit—the
optimism, the dogged determination, the fearlessness—will help
see you through the early years of business ownership, regardless
of whether your business is a franchise. But true entrepreneurs,
with their determination to do everything their own way, will rue
the day they decided to leave the workforce only to replace it with
the yoke of a franchisor. Decide which you are before proceeding
further.

You Are Not Getting Married

I often hear people refer to the franchise relationship as if it were a
marriage or a partnership. You should dissuade yourself of this notion from day one.

Despite lingering Victorian attitudes, a marriage is a relationship
between equals. In a marriage, you negotiate who mows the lawn,
who cleans the house, what side of the bed you will sleep on, and
what to watch on TV.

But in franchising, there is little negotiation and even less
equality between the parties. The franchisor owns the trademark
and other intellectual property and writes the contract. And the
franchisor makes the rules (which are generally housed in the
franchise agreement and the operations manual).

As such, the franchise relationship is much more akin to a parent-
child relationship. Typically, the new franchisee is highly dependent
on the franchisor early on. As the franchisee demonstrates her ability
to run the business, the franchisor may visit her less frequently and

provide less support. And as the franchisee gains more experience, she may try to stretch her wings a little, at which point it is the franchisor's job to be sure she understands that ultimately, as my mother used to say, "When you are living in my house, you play by my rules."

THE BOTTOM LINE: DON'T KID YOURSELF

We all allow our perceptions of ourselves and of the world around us to influence our decisions. And in the process, we all tell ourselves little lies.

These lies generally don't hurt anyone. But when it comes to buying a business, you need to be scrupulously and brutally honest in your answers to every question. If the fib you tell yourself is "I'm not an entrepreneur," and you are, when you buy that franchise, you may find that you're in for a 20-year battle with your franchisor—if you last that long. If you tell yourself, "I'm well-suited to business ownership," and you're not, you're probably headed for the hospital—hopefully to treat your ulcers and not a heart attack. If you tell yourself, "I can perform as well as the next guy, even if I'm inexperienced," and you can't, you may be headed for the poorhouse.

Perhaps the clearest manifestation of this is seen when estimating financial performance. For example, if a franchisor provides a Financial Performance Representation (FPR) (more on these in Chapter 7) in their disclosure document, you might be inclined to look at performance by quartile (if that is broken out) and do your business planning on the assumption that you will land in the top quartile.

But remember, that bell curve was made up entirely of people the franchisor chose because they believed they would outperform the average person. And each of them had something you lack—experience.

So how can you tell if you're being honest with yourself? There's no sure-fire way, but more than a little introspection is in order. Take a look at the questions in Figure 2–1 on page 30, and give some serious thought to the answers. After you finish, go to some people who know you well—your spouse, your friends, and your co-workers—and encourage them to be brutal in their assessment of your strengths and weaknesses. They may know you better than you know yourself. Make a conscious effort throughout this process to avoid any preconceived notions.

If you're still interested in a franchise, read on. In the next chapter, we'll look at how you should narrow your search.

Figure 2–1. **Worksheet: Questions to Ask Yourself**

Before deciding to purchase a franchise, you should ask yourself some hard questions. In particular, ask:

1. What are your goals? Can you achieve them without business ownership?

   _____

   _____

2. How badly do you want to achieve those goals? _____

   _____

   _____

3. What is your tolerance for risk? Can you sleep nights knowing you have invested your life's savings in a business opportunity that could fail? _____

   _____

   _____

4. How much capital can you afford to risk? _____

   _____

   _____

5. What is the minimum amount of money that you could reasonably live on during a potentially prolonged startup period for your franchise? _____

   _____

   _____

Figure 2–1. **Worksheet: Questions to Ask Yourself**, continued

6. Is your family firmly behind you in your decision? Do you have adequate support mechanisms in place? _____

_____

_____

7. Are you willing to follow someone else's system, even if you do not agree with some of the decisions being made? _____

_____

_____

8. Are you willing to sacrifice in the short run to achieve your goals in the long run?

_____

_____

9. Are you willing to work long hours if need be, especially at first? _____

_____

_____

10. Are you a self-starter? Or do you need constant coaching and prodding?

_____

_____

11. How important is security to you? _____

_____

_____

12. Do you thrive under pressure? _____

_____

_____

Figure 2–1. **Worksheet: Questions to Ask Yourself**, continued

13. Are you willing to share your results and your experiences with the franchisor?

_____

_____

14. Do you have the necessary skills to run a business? Sales skills? People/leadership skills? Financial skills? Etc. _____

_____

_____

15. Are you an optimist? How quickly do you bounce back from setbacks? _____

_____

_____

16. Do you have the fire in the belly every business owner needs? _____

_____

_____

Chapter 3

UNDERSTANDING RISK

All business decisions involve an element of risk, whether you are running a startup, changing your job, or choosing a franchise. All involve potential financial and personal minefields. That said, deciding to become a franchisee comes with its own special set of considerations. Not only are you putting your personal finances and reputation on the line, but you're making a choice that might affect the franchisor, investors, and potential employees and vendors as well. That is why conducting a thorough risk assessment is a key element of choosing a franchise. As you begin to narrow your list of potential franchise opportunities, you should do all you can to identify sources of risk in your investment decision. Start by considering your tolerance for risk.

Evaluating Your Risk Tolerance

As I said above, risk is a necessary part of *every* business decision. In fact, one of the first concepts taught in business classes is the "risk-reward" paradigm. In short, it means the greater the reward, the greater the risk. This paradigm is often illustrated using a risk-reward diagram such as the one in Figure 3–1. As you can see from looking at the graph, the higher the reward you hope to achieve, the more you must risk.

In looking at any point along this graph, it's easy to see that lower risks will bring lower anticipated returns and higher risk will bring higher anticipated returns. But do not let the straight line fool you. The line represents the *average* anticipated return vs. *perceived* risk—so it is probably better to envision each point on the line as representing an average of many outcomes at any given level of risk.

Assuming each point represents an average, the returns for any given point on the risk-reward curve could have their own bell curve—something along the lines of Figure 3–2, on page 35.

Figure 3-1. **Risk-Reward Graph**

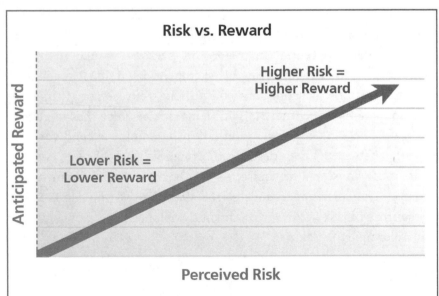

Figure 3-2. **Risk-Reward Bell Curves**

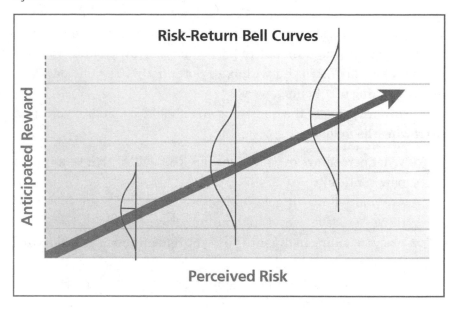

A graph such as this provides a somewhat deeper understanding, in that there is a range associated with the outcomes at every level of risk. Thus, the low-risk investment might, in fact, yield a higher return than a higher-risk investment. The point, of course, is that a high anticipated return does not mean the high return will actually materialize. In assessing your risk tolerance, therefore, you must start with the understanding that your investment may not work out.

There are at least two different categories of risk you should consider. On one hand, different franchise businesses will carry different levels of risk based on how well a particular concept does in a competitive marketplace. Think about Joe's Burgers vs. McDonald's and you will instantly understand the idea of concept risk. On the other hand, risk can also be quantified based on the total amount of money you devote to an investment. While the concept risk of a low-investment franchise might be similar to the concept risk of a high-investment franchise, from your perspective, you will be putting more dollars at risk with the latter.

Of course, there are other questions you should address in assessing your risk tolerance. For example, are you willing to risk your career by walking away from what might be a secure job (and which, at minimum, does not require you to invest capital) to start this new venture? Are you willing to potentially risk your personal life by working 60+ hours a week?

Below are some of the questions you should ask before you start narrowing the field:

> What percentage of your assets are you willing to invest in this new venture?
> Are you willing to give up the "security" (if there is such a thing in today's world) of your job when you get started?
> Are you willing to dip into your retirement funds to make your dream happen?
> Are you willing to work long hours and do whatever it takes to make your business succeed?
> Do you have a backup plan in case everything fails?
> Or are you ready, like Cortés, to scuttle your ships?

Once you understand your tolerance for risk, you will need to assess the potential risk of the various franchise investments you are considering to determine where they lie on the horizontal risk axis. Keep in mind their perceived risk is not limited to a single factor. Rather, it is the sum of all the risk factors that could cause your investment to go south. With that in mind, let's look at some of these risk factors so you can measure the risk associated with the franchises you are considering.

Fads

Start by asking the question of whether the concept is a fad. If it's been around for years and has an established market, it will probably be around in the future—absent other changes in the market. But if it's new to the market, be careful. Remember, new can often mean "higher risk." Franchise fads can allow you to make money, of course, especially if you jump in early (and perhaps get out early, too) or secure a location that gives you a captive market for a popular product. But be careful about jumping on any bandwagon if it seems faddish.

Fads are particularly perilous if there are low barriers to entry. If there are few intellectual property protections, it will be easier for competitors to enter the market. If there are low financial barriers to entry, this will make a proliferation of competition even more likely. Ultimately, the more competitors there are in a market (or the more there will be in the future), the greater your risk. So if your potential franchisor does not have a sustainable point of difference, consider whether you should include the "fad factor" in your risk calculation.

Regionality, Seasonality, and Predictability

You must also evaluate whether the concept will work well in your chosen market. Let's say you're from North Carolina and just love the local barbecue. When you relocate to Texas and see that there aren't any restaurants serving North Carolina-style barbecue, you may think there's a real opportunity—and maybe it is.

But perhaps there's a reason North Carolina barbecue isn't well-known in Texas. In North Carolina, barbecue means pulled pork on a bun with coleslaw. (The sauce varies depending on which part of the state you're from.) But in Texas, barbecue means BEEF with a spicy, tangy sauce. So while North Carolina barbecue *might* work in Texas, it could also be a very high-risk venture.

Cincinnati's five-way chili franchises (which I endorse heartily) provide yet another example. Two companies, Gold Star Chili and Skyline Chili, have done a wonderful job of popularizing this dish throughout Ohio, Kentucky, and Indiana—and Skyline has had some success in introducing it in Florida as well. It may be that these companies have just never tried to expand outside those markets— but it may also be that it is such a regional product that it would not succeed anywhere else. Why? Most people simply aren't used to the idea of chili served over spaghetti noodles—especially chili that is seasoned differently from how they make it at home. Remember, if it's new to a market, there's additional risk. Again, that's not necessarily a deal killer, but it's definitely something you should consider in your investment decision.

Likewise, consider the seasonality of a business. Some businesses will work better in warm climates and others in cold. Looking to get into a lawn-care business? Perhaps you will do better in Miami than you would in Chicago. Likewise, if you wanted to sell retail chocolates, you might anticipate being busiest during certain holidays (Christmas, Valentine's Day) and would perhaps do better in a not-so-humid climate.

There may, of course, be great reasons to consider one of these businesses. Perhaps you would like to work like a dog for nine months and spend the next three recovering and enjoying the fruits of your labor. That is a lifestyle goal with which few could argue. Or perhaps you see an opportunity to add a second seasonal business—say, a holiday décor business—to your lawn-care business so you can take advantage of the relationships you build (in which case be sure to read your in-term, noncompete clauses very carefully).

But seasonality poses a risk if you are not prepared for it. Labor losses from one season to the next can be an ongoing problem. And there will be the obvious need to manage cash flow during the fat months so you can survive during the lean ones. Lawn-care and holiday-lighting franchises are obvious examples that might marry well together. Tax-preparation businesses can anticipate a cycle of recruiting, training, and heavy production in the early months of the year, followed by a big drop in business in May. Bear in mind, a lot of businesses have less dramatic seasonal components that might not be apparent at first. Child-care and education businesses may be tied to the school year, for example. And a retail clothing business may require you to order inventory for the winter season six months before you start stocking it.

Closely related to the question of seasonality is the predictability of the cash flow in the business model. Some businesses build slowly over time but have a very strong base of repeat business. If you are in the temporary help business or the senior home-care market, for example, it may take weeks or even months before you generate your first client. But since the average client will require service over an extended period of time, the repeat nature of the business provides very predictable revenues (and ultimately profits) as the business grows. It is incumbent on the franchisee to start with an adequate capital reserve to sustain the business until they achieve cash-flow break-even.

Other businesses require their owners to constantly hunt for new clients. While a home-remodeling company, mortgage brokerage, or landscaping business may be very profitable, if it does not have a strong repeat business component, you will need to count on your franchisor's marketing expertise and your own sales skills to continue to grow the business.

Obviously, the more predictable the cash flow is over time, the easier it will be to manage your business—and the less risk you will incur in running it.

Concept and Market Shifts/Risks

Another thing to watch out for are potential changes in the marketplace caused by disruptive technology. Some years ago, I worked with Blockbuster Video, which had one of the better runs in the history of franchising. At one time, Blockbuster had close to 10,000 franchise locations worldwide. But with the advent of various pay-per-view services, the market changed dramatically. As I write this, there is only one store remaining—in Oregon (and who knows how long that one will hang on). After Dish Network's 2011 acquisition of the brand, almost all 1,700 remaining locations were shuttered, with the exception of a few in select markets, mostly in Alaska, and those finally closed in July 2018.

Another client, Florsheim Shoes, was hit by changes in the marketplace before it even started its franchise efforts. In the 1990s, almost every major mall in the U.S. boasted a Florsheim Shoe store, selling the iconic Florsheim wingtip shoe to what seemed like every American businessman. But around the turn of the 21st century,

Florsheim was hit with a double whammy. First, men stopped buying their shoes in malls. And second, U.S. companies seemed to go business casual almost overnight, which did not help a brand known for high-quality but very dressy shoes. Instead of expanding through franchising, Florsheim was forced to close stores and rethink its entire distribution strategy.

Another case is a company called ComputerLand, which opened in 1976. When ComputerLand first entered the marketplace, franchises were being snapped up by eager franchisees who wanted to cash in on the growing consumer market for home computers. Even their exorbitant franchise fee of $100,000 didn't do much to slow the pace of franchise sales, which for a time were being made at a rate of a sale a week. The company grew to more than 800 franchises in less than a decade. But as the demand for computers continued to grow, more and more manufacturers joined the marketplace, and prices for PCs began to drop dramatically—along with the margins retailers could charge for their products.

ComputerLand, with its 8 percent royalty, just couldn't survive in the new marketplace. Eventually, its franchisees revolted. The company eventually restructured its franchise offering, but its business model had become obsolete, and it closed forever in 1999.

So how could one predict problems like this? Well, an astute observer would note that virtually every product introduced into the consumer electronics field has been beset by strong price and margin competition. For example, when first introduced, a very basic pocket calculator sold for more than $100; an app that performs the same function is included on most smartphones today for free. Compact disc players and VCRs that once sold in excess of $1,000 per unit rapidly became less expensive to replace than fix. Today there is an entire generation that probably wouldn't recognize them if they saw one. What has happened historically will often happen again. If your franchisor has a commodity-type product—or one that could become commoditized in the future—factor that into the risk equation.

Market risks are different from concept risks in that they reflect things happening outside the franchise in question. They might include competitive strategies, changes in market demand, or changes in the market as a whole.

Ask yourself whether there are any trends in the marketplace that could negatively affect demand for the franchisor's services. For instance, if you are considering a McDonald's franchise, ask yourself if there is a noticeable consumer trend toward eating healthier. You might also be concerned with the aging of the U.S. population, as that might mean proportionately fewer young customers—a market that McDonald's targets aggressively.

Are there any potential threats that could reduce the demand for your product? For example, if you were interested in a burger restaurant, you might be concerned about an outbreak of E.coli, such as the 1993 incident at Jack in the Box, which nearly had a devastating effect on the chain. Or consider what happened to Meineke when manufacturing improvements in mufflers forced the company to pivot to complete car care. While Meineke was able to reinvent itself, perhaps your chosen franchisor will not be so swift to respond. What is the potential that a substitute product could come along and capture significant market share? If you are considering a franchise selling print advertising, could online advertising reduce your opportunity—or can your franchisor adapt to the new world? Does your franchisor have truly proprietary knowledge? Do its patents really protect its process entirely?

So where are the obvious market shifts today? My crystal ball is no better than yours, but I would suggest you try to understand how ecommerce and the internet might impact a franchise's business model before investing. If you think change is coming with the emergence of the Millennial marketplace, you should factor that into your thinking as well.

Regulations

In addition to market shifts, government regulation poses a potential threat. While it's tough to prognosticate what the government will do, there are certainly some things on the horizon.

One obvious example is franchising in the emerging market for cannabis and related products. At the moment, the pendulum is swinging in favor of more broad-based acceptance of cannabis retailing—at least at the state level. A retail cannabis franchise could certainly offer a significant opportunity, and franchisors in that space could provide substantial value to their franchisees when it comes to things like product sourcing, marketing, legal compliance, and operational systems. At the same time, cannabis franchises must still navigate federal laws; banking regulations are one major hurdle right now. And conceivably, regulations could be enacted at the federal level that could end recreational cannabis retailing overnight.

Risky? Sure. But cannabis is an area that potentially offers high rewards to those interested in franchising.

It's ultimately up to you to predict what might happen in any market. You may not be able to precisely quantify the amount of risk, but you should do your best to understand it and decide whether you can live with it. If anything on your list looks too risky for your tolerance level, draw a line through it and move on.

Competition and Barriers to Entry

In the early 1980s, companies like TCBY (The Country's Best Yogurt) began franchising a unique new concept—stores that specialized in soft-serve frozen yogurt. While these stores had some immediate success, a wary franchise buyer would have seen a number of signs that this was a high-risk situation.

Obviously, the concept itself was new, which sometimes means increased risk. But there were other problems as well. TCBY and the other yogurt chains sold one product that might turn out to be a fad. But there was a bigger problem still—one intrinsic to the concept itself.

With an initial investment of perhaps $100,000, TCBY was created as a low-cost-of-entry franchise. It wasn't long before numerous competitors sprang up: All American Ice Cream & Frozen

Yogurt, California Yogurt, Everything Yogurt, Freshëns Premium Yogurt, Yo! Frooty, Heidi's Frogen Yozurt, I Can't Believe It's Yogurt, J. Higby's Yogurt Shop, Love's Yogurt, Yogurt Naturally, Penguin's Frozen Yogurt, Tastes Yogurt Emporium, Yogurt Fantastik Frozen Yogurt Stores, The Yogurt Station, Yogurty's Yogurt Discovery, Yogen Früz, Yummy-Yogurt, Zack's Famous Frozen Yogurt, and more.

The proliferation of yogurt shops was only the start of the problem. It wasn't long before the big players in the ice cream business began offering yogurt as well. Baskin-Robbins started serving yogurt in many of their stores. Bresler's Ice Cream even renamed their stores Bresler's Ice Cream & Yogurt Shops. There was instant competition from thousands of locations.

A typical frozen yogurt franchise had only product differentiation to attract customers. But how different was their product?

The central problem was that the industry had very low barriers to entry. Not only was it easy for competing concepts to arise, but non-yogurt food-service operators could add a comparable product with only a few thousand dollars and 12 square feet of floor space, creating even more competition.

There was, of course, a consolidation phase in the marketplace, during which a number of franchisors were either acquired or closed shop. TCBY and Yogen Früz prospered. A few others survived but failed to grow significantly. And a number of franchisors simply went away.

Fast-forward to 2005. Along comes a company called Pinkberry, which began franchising a tart frozen yogurt product with some minor variations on the service concept. Shortly thereafter, it was joined by Red Mango, Menchie's, sweetFrog, Orange Leaf, Yogurtland, and a host of smaller competitors. The yogurt wars began in earnest all over again.

This is not to say that these companies are completely undifferentiated, or that they do not deserve your investment. There are yogurt franchises that are still driving great numbers—perhaps because of their location and due at least in part to the intellectual property given to them by their franchisors.

But it illustrates that when you purchase a franchise, you may be looking at a 20-year investment—or even longer. And during that time frame, you can and should anticipate that there will be changes in the competitive landscape.

So ask potential franchisors about the barriers to competitive entry. Do they have proprietary products or technology? Is there a steep learning curve associated with the industry? Are there issues relative to licensing or accreditation that will reduce competition? Is there a shortage of people with the experience to succeed in this field (and does this work for or against you)? The higher the barriers, the lower the risk of future competition. Ask yourself how much it would cost a company to gain the knowledge, expertise, and assets your franchisor has and how quickly they could do so.

Then ask if anyone has those assets now and who would gain the most by entering this market. Are there any major corporations that would strengthen their core businesses significantly by doing so? If there are, that threat must also be assessed. Patents are a tremendous asset—unless the franchisor cannot protect them. No market is impenetrable. The best you can hope for is a sustainable advantage.

When examining any potential franchise, you need to ask yourself not only who your current competitors are, but who will be your competitors over the next 10 to 20 years. Who wants in? Who has easy access to this market? Is there an 800-pound gorilla sitting on the sidelines that could easily jump into your market and disrupt your industry?

Does the franchise you are considering have proprietary technology, recipes, or anything else that will increase barriers to entry? Are their trade secrets really secrets? Try to figure out who stands to win and who stands to lose if trends continue, and then try to figure out what the losers will do.

Ask if the market is fully developed or in its infancy. The "younger" a market is, the more risk is associated with every company in that market. If you think an industry is getting overbuilt or may be subject to new competitive pressures, factor that into your risk equation.

This occurred in the quick lube industry a couple of decades ago. Early in the market's development, quick lubes often serviced 55 or more cars per day, but as more and more competitors entered the marketplace, these facilities saw their car counts (and their profits) fall dramatically.

Look at the competitive landscape and ask yourself if your franchisor is the dominant competitor in the market. Are they in second place? If it is a new market, can they achieve a dominant position? If not, have they carved out a defensible niche? Is there a competitor or potential competitor that is so dominant as to be capable of winning a price war or otherwise have a significant negative impact on your business?

This should all be factored into your assessment of risk.

Recession Resistance

Another question you will want to address is how well the business will hold up under different economic circumstances. Some businesses perform better than others in difficult times.

The first thing that might come to mind is the degree to which a business concept involves a discretionary purchase. For example, if your customers were to lose their jobs, they might be less likely to have their carpets cleaned, their houses painted, or their cars washed, as these tasks could be put off (or done by the consumers themselves) if they had to tighten their belts. Some businesses are highly recession-resistant, such as funeral parlors, health care, and education—although in each case, the consumer may reduce their spending on these services. And some businesses will actually thrive during tough times. A consumer may be more likely to repair his car during a recession, whereas in a good economy he might simply buy a new one.

You must also understand that not all businesses that thrive during a recession will do well when the economy is rolling along. Consider, for example, a mortgage brokerage franchise that focuses on refinancing. In a recession, when interest rates are falling, that business might make significant profits on the many consumers taking advantage of the low rates to refinance their homes. But when interest rates once again begin to rise as the economy heats up, refinancing could virtually disappear, leaving the franchisee to compete only in the new loan origination side of the business.

Making this call is not always as intuitive as it might seem. Some businesses that offer a small indulgence might do well in recessionary times, as people choose to "trade down" with their buying habits. For example, while high-end and mid-priced restaurants might falter during hard times, fast-food operations and bakeries might hold steady or even prosper. So be sure to ask any franchisors you are considering how the business fares under different economic conditions.

Big vs. Small Franchise Companies

The longer a franchisor has been in business and the more successful locations it operates, the more refined you would expect the system to be. The bigger the support team is, the more resources you will have to draw on. While this is often the case, it would also be fairly easy to point to some large franchise companies that, possibly because of their fast growth, saw a significant number of franchise closures over a relatively short period of time. Consider these examples:

✂ The women-only fitness center Curves was reported to have some 10,000 franchise locations in 2006—one of the fastest franchisors ever to achieve that lofty height. As of this writing, the company boasts 4,000 locations. While many of those 4,000 franchisees may be very successful, the loss of 6,000 franchises in a bit more than a decade raises the question of what happened.

✂ Similarly, sandwich chain Quiznos saw very rapid growth, with more than 5,000 locations by 2007. Again, a huge chain by franchising standards. While it remains a huge chain, it had just over 2,000 locations in 2018.

✂ Going back a little farther in history, one of the biggest early success stories in franchising, Howard Johnson's restaurants, with their iconic orange roofs, were once the largest restaurant chain in the U.S., with more than 1,000 locations. Today, Howard Johnson hotels remain (now owned by Wyndham Hotels), but there is only one restaurant still standing, in Lake George, New York.

And, of course, there are other large franchise systems that have had similar declines over the years. So while bigger franchisors may have "figured it out" and will certainly have more resources to provide support, size is not necessarily an antidote to risk.

On the other side of the spectrum, smaller, younger franchisors probably will not have the resources from a support perspective. Their track record may be shorter. But that does not mean they should be eliminated from consideration. Choosing a small franchisor may allow you to get in on the cutting edge of the newest trend. Our client Massage Envy started franchising only months after opening their doors for business—and gave many of their early franchisees the opportunity to earn millions. It was a young, small brand that experienced exponential franchise growth early on and is now one of the biggest names in franchising.

Investing in a younger franchisor may actually have other advantages as well. For example, a younger franchisor will give you access to the most lucrative markets, where the risk of failure may actually be lower. Likewise, while their staff may not be as big, you may have the opportunity to work directly with the founder of the franchise company, instead of a young hire with less hands-on experience. While you should certainly consider size and experience in your risk equation, a large franchisor with an outdated business model may actually be riskier than a younger franchisor on the cutting edge of the latest trend.

Capital Risks

Capital (or financial) risks are involved when the franchisor does not have the resources to meet its growth plans. You will want to closely examine the financial statements in the franchise disclosure document (FDD) to determine just how well-capitalized the franchisor is. (If you are not well-versed in finance, ask your accountant to help. An hour of their time now could save you a great deal of grief later.) We will go into the FDD in greater detail in Chapter 5.

Look at several different measures of the company's financial health before deciding whether to become a franchisee. These financial ratios, which are commonly used in evaluating income statements and balance sheets, measure different elements of business health. *Liquidity measures* (such as the ratio of current assets to current liabilities) will help you gauge the franchisor's ability to meet its current obligations. *Leverage ratios* (such as the ratio of debt to equity) will help you gauge the franchisor's relative level of risk. But the big questions are whether the franchisor has set aside adequate capital for growth and whether it is running profitably.

So start by determining the franchisor's *net worth*. To do this, find the total assets in the balance sheet (which is included in the FDD) and subtract the total liabilities. This should give you a feel for the amount of assets the franchisor has at its disposal to meet its ongoing obligations. In calculating this number, however, be sure you understand the nature of the assets in question. For example, if one of the assets is goodwill (which typically refers to the premium paid over book value if a business has been acquired), realize that it cannot be used to pay the bills. Again, if you are not familiar with accounting practices, you will want to hire someone to help you conduct this analysis.

The second thing you want to look at closely is the franchisor's *profitability*. This can be easily determined by looking at the franchisor's income statement. But again, you need to examine it more closely. One indication that the franchisor has achieved a level of stable profitability is the degree to which it has achieved royalty self-sufficiency. Franchise fees may come and go, but royalties provide a predictable source of revenue from year to year. So if you back franchise fees out of the income statement, a more mature franchisor should still show a profit.

However, there are a couple of complications you should be aware of. First, almost all new franchisors will elect to form a separate company to act as the franchisor entity. Some want to limit their liability. Others want to keep their corporate financial statements confidential. Still others want to avoid a more complex audit process. Unfortunately, this will block you from seeing the financial statements of affiliated entities. Often, all that will show up on an opening balance sheet for a new franchisor will be the initial capital contribution—leaving you in the dark as to whether the company has access to more capital should the need arise.

Second, the way in which franchisors choose to disclose revenue on their income statements can vary from company to company. Some lump franchise fees together with royalties (and perhaps other fees) under a broad heading of "Franchise Fees," leaving you in the dark on the question of royalty self-sufficiency.

Thus, in order to get a complete financial picture, you should run a Dun & Bradstreet credit report on both the franchisor *and any affiliated companies* (we'll have more information on this in Chapter 5). Your banker can do this on your behalf. And again, speak with your accountant if you have problems understanding the results.

Management Risks

Good management can overcome almost any risk factor you've read about in this chapter. Good management can find capital when necessary, roll with the punches, and take a mediocre concept and make it succeed. But there is no cure for bad management. Bad management will take even the best concept and make it fail.

So how do you identify good management? The FDD is a good place to start. It will reflect how long the franchisor's management team has been in place. It will tell you the breadth of experience and how much industry-specific experience each member of management has. It will reveal whether the company has a history of bankruptcy or litigation.

In addition to reviewing the FDD, you should ask existing franchisees about management, read any available industry publications, and look at management's track record. If the management team has been together for a while, how has the organization been doing from a financial perspective? From a growth perspective? What is their credit rating? Does management have a history of growing a business and then selling it off? Or are they in it for the long haul?

We will discuss your assessment of the management team in more detail in Chapters 5 and 6. Just keep in mind in the meantime that management is the single most important component to the success of almost every business.

THE BOTTOM LINE: USE MURPHY'S LAW TO NARROW YOUR LIST

You will not find a business that is completely risk-free, so give up on that notion now. The key to your success is to understand the risks you are taking and use that knowledge to make informed business decisions.

In this chapter, I have outlined some of the most common risks you may encounter in franchising. But perhaps the greatest risk is the one you could not anticipate. The road in front of your operation closes. A partner dies. An illness strikes. The market for your products or services suddenly shifts. You face an acrimonious divorce. A random act of terror drives people away from shopping in malls, where your franchise is located. The list of possible risks is long and ever-expanding.

Some of these risks are personal, not business-related, but you may encounter them nonetheless. In considering any franchise, ask yourself what could possibly go wrong and factor that into your risk equation.

Chapter 4

NARROWING THE FIELD

O nce you assess your personality and run various risk assessments, you can start narrowing your list to those franchises that you think will be the best fit. Not to muddy the waters, but the possibilities truly are endless: From small service franchises and homebased options to restaurants and large retail operations, there is a franchise in just about every flavor. As we have already discussed, there are no reliable statistics on the number of franchise systems in the U.S. Despite that, most industry experts estimate there are somewhere in the area of 4,000 or more active franchisors in the marketplace. So how do you narrow thousands of possibilities down to the one perfect franchise for you? Like anything else in life or business, you need a good strategy.

Using a "Goals-Oriented" Approach

Start with a basic understanding of why you are buying a franchise in the first place. A franchise is not an impulse purchase—or at least it shouldn't be. It is an investment you're making in order to reach certain goals.

If you wish to accomplish a goal, you must first understand that goal. That sounds logical, but you'd be surprised how many people purchase franchises based on emotion. Buying a Jersey Mike's franchise just because you love subs probably isn't a good idea, for example. But if you see a need in your local sub sandwich marketplace, run the risk assessments, and discover that the need you can fill with that franchise is in alignment with your goals, you may have a winner.

So how do you make the goals-oriented approach work for you? The first and most important step in the process is to make some personal assessments before narrowing the field.

Create a Goal Map

Think of the process of selecting a franchise as a road trip to a new and distant destination. Maybe you're stuck in Chicago in January and want to go to a nice, high-end beach resort for a couple of weeks of well-deserved rest and relaxation. You know warmer weather lies to the south and know which roads head in that direction. And perhaps you can keep heading that way as you travel by the position of the sun. But what are the odds that you will find exactly what you were looking for when you set off on your journey?

Given how precious our vacation time is, I expect most of us would start by choosing our destination. What do we want that resort to be like? Do we want the attractions of a major city or the tranquility of an isolated location? Should it have fine dining or be more casual? Should it have golf and a spa, or more kid-friendly amenities? Remember, we only have two weeks, including travel time by car, which limits how far away it can be. And, of course, we have a limited budget to spend on the trip.

Once you have determined your criteria and chosen your destination, all you have to do is plug it into your car's navigation system, and you'll know the fastest way to get there and how to avoid traffic and other obstacles along the way.

The same is true of your franchise purchase. It is important to have a good understanding of your starting point. But beyond that, you need to know where the journey will take you, the distance you need to travel, the time it will take, and your budget for the trip.

As a starting point, decide what you hope to achieve with your franchise purchase. Ask yourself where you want to be and how soon you need to arrive there—whether it be 5, 10, or 20 years from now. Here are some self-reflective questions you can ask:

✂ What do I want out of life?

✂ What am I willing to give up?

✂ Do I want to make millions and accumulate generational wealth, or will a nice income suffice?

✂ Is it independence I seek?

✂ Do I want stature in the community?

✂ Do I just want to pursue a more personally satisfying career?

✂ Do I want to cash out of the business after five years? If so, for how much?

✂ Am I looking to retire to the Bahamas?

✂ Am I looking for a business I can build and then pass on to my heirs?

Once you've answered these questions, you need to quantify your answers. All too often, I speak to business owners who state goals like, "I want to grow as fast as I can without sacrificing quality, and then sell the business." While that might seem like a worthy goal, in reality, it is not a goal at all. In the best-case scenario, you could call it a philosophy. In the worst case, you might say they were ducking the question.

For a proper analysis, you need to quantify very specifically your *MINIMAL* financial goals and the time frame over which you want to achieve them. Don't let yourself off the hook. Ask yourself how much you want to make when you sell your business. A million dollars? Two million? Ten million? How much is an adequate income? Set some minimum aspirations against which you can measure your strategy for achieving or exceeding that goal. If you want to keep the business, you need to decide how much you want to take out each year.

One exercise I have used with business owners is what I call my blank check test. Assuming you want to sell the business, imagine someone is standing in front of you with a magic checkbook, willing to write you a postdated check for any amount you say. The terms: You will sell the business to them at a specific point in time for the amount on the check. Once you receive the check, you will immediately put it in an envelope and forget you have it. And up until the date on the check, you will work just as hard as you would have if you did not have it. You will have all the sleepless nights, sweat all the payrolls, suffer all the employee headaches, miss all the vacations, and work like a dog to accomplish something. And you must decide today—in fact, right now—or the buyer will walk away faster than a frustrated Mark Cuban on *Shark Tank*. What is your *absolutely lowest* acceptable selling price? What are the next five (or whatever) years of your life worth to you?

Once you know that number, it is relatively simple to calculate what that business would need to be earning to sell for that amount. For a small business, a simple rule of thumb is that a purchase price of five times earnings would provide the new owner with a 20 percent rate of return—so divide your selling price by five, and you can project the level of earnings needed to give you a reasonable chance at achieving that price.

If, on the other hand, you want to hold on to your business and pass it on to your heirs, ask yourself how much money you need to earn to live the lifestyle you dream about. This might take a little time, but think about the house you want, the cars you want, the lives you want for your children—and put together a budget. How much do you need to "have it all," and how soon do you need to have it?

The purpose of these goals, of course, is to give us a destination. But if things go well, there is no rule saying that our final destination cannot surpass our minimal dreams.

Consider Your Capital

When it comes to capital, how much is enough? The answer is simple: more than you need. While that might seem flippant, consider this: More startup businesses fail because of undercapitalization than for any other reason—probably by a factor of ten.

So where do you start? You need to determine how much you *can* invest and how much you are *willing* to invest. You might find those two numbers are different.

First, how much *can* you invest? The answer lies in your net worth. To determine that, you should create your own personal balance sheet.

There are a number of places where you can download a personal balance sheet template that you can populate in Excel (or by hand) with your own information. Start by adding up all your assets to determine how much you own: cash, checking accounts, investments, home value, personal property, retirement accounts, business interests, and other assets of value. Next add up everything you owe (called liabilities): credit card debt, mortgage debt, and other loans. The difference between what you own and what you owe is your net worth. (There is a sample balance sheet included in the confidential information request form in Appendix C.)

Your net worth figure represents an approximation of the capital available for you to invest in a franchise. You must next decide how much of that you are willing to risk on the franchise.

The amount of capital you are willing to risk is not necessarily the same as the amount you have to invest. You may choose to invest only a fraction of your net worth in the franchise, or you may choose to invest more using the sometimes dangerous magic of *leverage*.

Leverage Is Like Wine—Wonderful if You Know Your Limit

In quantifying how much you are willing to risk, you must understand the concept of leverage. Leverage, or your ability to use borrowed money for an investment, is like wine—it's great in the right quantity, but too much can kill you. While leverage increases your potential return, it also increases your risk.

To understand the power of leverage, let's use the everyday example of buying a home. If you were to purchase a $200,000 home today, you might be able to buy it with 10 percent down. With monthly payments of perhaps $900 per month (without taxes and insurance), you figure you can afford it, because you and your spouse each take home $2,000 per month.

Over the next three years, let's say you increase your paid-in principal by about $9,000. Thus, the average equity you have in that home will be a little over $24,500.

If you then decide to sell the home, the selling price is dictated based on the market, regardless of your equity position. Thus, if real estate has been booming, you may be able to sell your property for $230,000. Without factoring in closing costs or commissions for the sake of this analysis, your three-year return on your total investment of $200,000 is around 15 percent. But your three-year return on the $24,500 in average equity you invested will be $30,000/$24,500— or about 122 percent!

That's great news, but things don't always work out that well. Anything can happen, from unexpected medical bills to natural disasters. What if you or your spouse is laid off? Can you still afford that home on only $2,000 a month?

Let's change the scenario and assume for a moment that you put down 50 percent instead of 10 percent on this same house. Your monthly payment is now reduced to about $500. And since your payments are $400 less, you can survive if one of you is out of work. But if you sell your home, your return on equity will be substantially reduced—you will still earn the same return on investment, but your average equity would be about $30,000/$102,500—or a three-year return of 29 percent.

Now assume you paid cash for your home, with no payments and no risk of bank foreclosure. But your return on equity is now reduced to 15 percent for the three-year period. As you can see, risk (as measured by leverage) and return are directly related.

Apply this same principle to your investment in a franchise. Perhaps you have a net worth of $500,000. But since a lot of your capital might be tied up in your home and retirement savings, you only have $100,000 to invest in your franchise. You will need to decide whether to leverage yourself into a higher investment with a higher potential return.

So how much is too much?

There are two factors influencing the answer to that question. The first is you—how much of an appetite for risk do you have? Remember, your banker is going to take a security interest in your assets. So even though you invested $100,000 of your capital out of pocket, if your franchise business fails, they may go after your house or other assets. While your equity investment may only be $100,000, your total investment will include the money lent to you by your bank.

The second part of this equation is your banker or other lender. Generally speaking, bankers and/or Small Business Administration (SBA) lenders like *at least* 30 percent of the initial investment to come from your personal equity. So conceivably, you could leverage a $100,000 investment up to $300,000 or so.

Of course, it is never quite that easy. Your ability to leverage your investment will be dictated by a variety of factors:

- ✄ any collateral you can offer in the business
- ✄ anticipated cash flows
- ✄ your credit score
- ✄ other sources of income (e.g., passive income or spouse's earnings)
- ✄ your banker's opinion of the franchise
- ✄ your banker's opinion of *you* as a franchisee

In other words, you probably won't be able to pin down an exact number, but you should have a general understanding of how much you can invest before you go too far with your search.

Meet with Your Banker

One step you can take early in the process is to speak candidly with your banker. While you will certainly need to have a more detailed conversation once you have chosen your franchise, your banker (or several bankers, if you have the time to speak to more than one) can give you a great idea of acceptable risk. Before the meeting, create a personal balance sheet—a detailed accounting of your personal assets and liabilities. On the assets side, include anything you own that could help fund your business. In addition to savings, itemize the value of your stocks, bonds, retirement funds, your home, and any other investments you might be able to leverage. On the liabilities side, itemize any mortgages or other loans.

Then develop a list of any income you can count on while getting started in your own business. If, for example, your spouse will continue to work, the banker will want to know how much he or she will be earning. The banker will also want to know what your ongoing expenses will be during that period, so include any mortgage payments, car payments, and living expenses in this analysis.

Of course, at this stage, the one thing you cannot show them is your projected earnings or the operating costs of the franchise. Bring what you have to your banker and ask for advice on how much you could reasonably afford to borrow. They will not, of course, commit to a loan at this point, but they should be able to give you an order of magnitude as to where your total investment level might lie.

Bankers ultimately want your business, so going to them early will help you in two ways: It will show the banker that you value their advice and demonstrate your sound business judgment—which may help you when you actually do go to them for the loan. And second, it will help you understand how much leverage you can actually afford.

Once you have met with your banker and have a good feel for your available capital, your risk tolerance, and your ability to leverage your way into a franchise, you are ready to begin the screening process to help you narrow the field. The first and easiest screen to employ is the size of investment. As you begin researching franchise companies, you should immediately rule out any franchises that are above the top of your investment range.

The required investment for a franchise can be found in various online portals, franchise directories, the franchisor's collateral materials, or in Item 7 of a franchisor's FDD (more on this in Chapter 5). These investment figures are typically expressed as a range, with the low end representing a best-case scenario and the high end hopefully representing a worst-case scenario. If you want to be cautious, you will probably want to have more available capital than the high end of the range, as one of the biggest causes of failed businesses is undercapitalization. In fact, you may even want to have some contingency funds set aside in case you exceed the worst-case projection.

If you are more of a risk taker, you may still want to consider investments where your available capital falls within, but not above the top of, the investment range. If you choose one of these franchises, you should be very sure you understand the parameters of the investment and have *very specific reasons* to believe you will be at or near the low end of the investment range. If your rationale for anticipating a best-case scenario is limited to the care you will take with your investment dollars, you are probably letting your emotions get the better of you.

How Does It Fit on You?

Over the years, I have been asked numerous times why certain franchise concepts failed.

Failure hides behind many excuses and takes many forms. A downturn in the economy. Undercapitalization. A change in consumer tastes. New and stronger competition. The loss of a key employee. A shortage of working capital. Even a hurricane or a flood. But when you consider all the things that can go wrong, the single most important factor in the success of any business is good management.

Good management will prepare for changes in the economy, motivate and retain key employees, and plan for worst-case scenarios and other disasters. Good management will ensure it knows the market and is prepared for new competition and changes in consumer tastes. Good management will not allow the business to expand beyond the capacity of its capital base or will raise additional capital for growth.

But there is no cure for bad management.

Since we're talking about purchasing a franchise here, chances are you have already selected the key person in your management team—you. Hopefully, you already have some of the basic knowledge you need to run a business. And if you choose the right franchise, the franchisor will teach you everything else you need to know.

Since the top management won't be changing, you need to be sure that the management fits the franchise. Thus, this filter is fairly simple: Eliminate any categories of business opportunities that you do not enjoy and that do not fit your management style.

All too often I am asked, "What is a good franchise?" But when I dig deeper, I find the real question is where someone can make the most money. This is the wrong question.

Remember, this franchise is something you will be doing almost every day of your life for the next 10, 20, or maybe even 30 years. Does it seem fun? Does it incorporate elements you enjoy? Are you passionate about the products you'd be selling or the services you'd be providing?

Yes, I know that earlier in this book I talked about the dangers of making an emotional decision when purchasing a franchise. And the question, "Will I have fun?" may sound trivial and emotionally charged, but it is actually critical from several perspectives. First, it's important to enjoy your life. If you're choosing something to do for the next 20 years, you'd better like it. But from a business perspective, it is important to determine if you will be able to sustain the effort needed to make any business succeed in the long term. In other words, it answers the question, "Will I have the stamina?"

When you get started in business, you may find yourself working long days and weekends for months, or even years, at a time. Doing something you love will get you through those long days.

And while you're at it, try to eliminate businesses for which you have no talent. The market for accounting services may be exploding, but if you don't have a head for numbers, you should probably avoid these franchises. Chances are that if you don't have this proficiency, you don't enjoy it—and even counting all your money won't take away the boredom of a job you hate.

Ask questions like:

- ✂ What suits my temperament?
- ✂ Am I a better salesperson than an administrator?
- ✂ Do I get along well with people?
- ✂ Do I work well in groups?
- ✂ Do I prefer to work on my own?
- ✂ Am I self-motivated?
- ✂ Am I a leader?
- ✂ Am I good at management?
- ✂ Can I manage a workforce made up of part-time workers who may turn over at a high rate?
- ✂ How well do I handle rejection?
- ✂ What hours do I want to work—or does that matter?
- ✂ Is it important for me to have an office or a business that is separate from my home life?

These questions are a good jumping-off point for further self-reflection. One of the hardest tasks we must set for ourselves is to objectively evaluate our own strengths and weaknesses. Knowing what you're good at will help narrow the field even more. If that means you have to eliminate some brand-name franchisors or some hot new concepts, so be it. Just because they're right for other franchisees doesn't make them right for you.

If you have already decided on an industry—for instance, if you have 30 years of restaurant experience and now want to buy a restaurant franchise—you may want to skip this step, but only if you really know what you're getting into.

As you go through this process, be brutal. Slash entire industries off your list. Cut companies that don't match your profile or aren't franchising in your area. By the time you get to Chapter 5, you will be ready to get down to a detailed examination of the few remaining companies.

Developing Your "Short List"

As mentioned earlier, there are approximately 4,000 franchisors in the U.S. today, and that number is growing by several hundred every year. Moreover, franchisors can be found in virtually every field of business. Of course, there are franchise restaurants and franchise retail stores, but there are also franchise sales forces and franchise service businesses. There are even franchise medical services. So how do you come up with your short list of a few franchises worthy of closer investigation?

First, put together your franchise universe by assembling a longer list of all likely contenders. The logical place to start is the internet.

When I first started working in the franchise world, the only way to sort through the universe of franchises was to purchase various print directories that would list many, but not all, franchise opportunities. The turn of the century saw the advent of online franchise portals, which serve as advertising vehicles and typically do not include information on nonadvertisers. Many of these portals are searchable by industry, geography, investment, etc., giving you a great place to start. Appendix A at the end of the book has a list of franchise portals.

As is always the case with the internet, these portals change their format with some degree of regularity. Portals list their franchises differently (for example, one portal might have a category for medical franchises, while another might categorize them as health care). And none of the portals contains a comprehensive list of every franchise offered. So you will likely need to go through this exercise several times on different portals.

At the time of this writing, some of the more comprehensive portals include:

✂ Entrepreneur's Franchise Hub (https://www.entrepreneur.com/franchises)
✂ Franchise Direct (https://www.franchisedirect.com/)
✂ Franchise Gator (https://www.franchisegator.com/)

✄ IFA Popular Franchise Opportunities (https://www.franchise.org/search-by-franchisor)

✄ FranchiseOpportunities.com (https://www.franchiseopportunities.com/)

✄ BizBuySell (https://www.bizbuysell.com/)

This is the slash and burn phase of your search, in which you develop your short list of possible franchises. Essentially, you want to use a successive series of finer and finer filters to narrow your list of companies under consideration to a handful—two dozen at most.

So, let's start slashing.

Only Fools Fall in Love with the Product

Your first round of slashing must include an honest discussion with yourself about exactly what you're buying. For many franchisees, that "what" is not so much a thing as a feeling. If you ask an experienced franchise salesperson what sells franchises, they will tell you it's emotion—particularly for first-time business owners.

I once heard a story of how Popeyes sold a franchise to a doctor who had been eating their chicken for years. Apparently, he had recently moved and loved Popeyes' food so much that he had to have a restaurant in his new hometown—even if he had to buy it himself. At least the doctor was apparently happy with his decision, but many franchisees are not so lucky. They fall in love with the product, buy the franchise, and then wonder why they don't succeed in business. Sure, the product you are selling is important. It should be something that isn't easily duplicated and, most important, it should be something the consumer will buy.

But when you buy a franchise, you are not buying the chicken, the fancy new vending machine, the bagel oven, or the virtual reality game. You are investing in a business system. You are investing in the support of the franchisor's management team. You are investing in the franchisor's track record and history of success. You are investing in their marketing system. You are investing in the future of their market. And you are investing in yourself.

If you are selling the cure for the common cold, but you don't have a good business system, you will fail. The best hamburger does not always win the race. The best business does.

Yes, you want to love what you are doing. But loving what you are doing is not the same as loving the product. Your focus needs to be on what you are buying (the business) and not on what your customer is buying (the chicken).

Supplement Your Research

Once you have determined that you do, in fact, want to invest in a business system and not a romantic idea of business ownership, you need to start researching potential franchises. While the internet is an extremely valuable resource in your hunt for potential franchises, there is no one source that can give you a comprehensive list of franchisors from which to choose. Some franchisors choose not to advertise on the internet. And while they may have a franchise tab on their websites, it may not always be obvious.

Moreover, the internet can never give you the same feel for a concept that you can get through other, more personal means. So before we move on, let's discuss some of your other options for information gathering.

The Franchisor

Of course, your first (and hopefully best) source of information on a franchise company will be the franchise company itself. It will typically be able to provide you with a wealth of information, including the FDD, franchise brochures or other promotional materials, links to franchisee testimonials, and perhaps information on the industry in general. If you are interested in a particular franchise, be sure to reach out to it directly.

For some, the experience of speaking with a salesman may seem uncomfortable and intimidating, and asking for all this information might feel overwhelming at first, but don't worry. In the best organizations, the franchise salespeople (who are generally called franchise development officers) are accustomed to working with people who may be new to the process and perhaps a little nervous. Most of these development officers will not be pushy or overly aggressive, but you can expect they will attempt to qualify you on the first call. Most will ask you to fill out a confidential information request form (CIRF) and discuss their process for mutual evaluation.

Typical qualifying questions will involve your capitalization, desired geographical region, and timetable for deciding. Assuming you are serious about investing in a franchise, you should be frank with your answers—under/overstating your available capital or pushing out your timeline may end the relationship prematurely. The franchise development officer will often then try to set an agenda, saying something like, "Our goal is to mutually determine if we have a fit. I expect that you have a lot of questions—as do I—but if we can get all of our questions answered in the next 12 weeks, will you be ready to make a decision one way or the other?" Assuming you answer yes, they will then often propose a series of steps you will both go through to learn more about each other. In the best organizations, these steps are designed to get you the information you need.

Some of the steps may include ones referenced throughout this book: a review call to go over the FDD, market visits, calls to franchisees, speaking to your banker, and investigating the market for your services. Take advantage of this resource as soon as you are down to your short list, even if this choreographed process seems somewhat contrived or artificial.

One other point: These franchise development officers often "give you permission to say 'no'" at any time during the process. The best ones encourage it; they don't want to spend their time chasing after you if you have already decided to move on. I would urge you to let them know as soon as you decide to cross them off your list. It will make their lives easier—or give them a chance to address your concerns.

Franchise Brokers

One of the resources that can help guide you through the process of buying a franchise is a franchise broker (also called a lead-referral network, or LRN). Brokers, who often call themselves "franchise consultants," can be a valuable tool in helping you assess your options. But before you decide to work with a broker, you should understand how their business model works.

Unlike a franchise salesperson, a broker is not limited to a single franchise concept. Instead, a typical franchise broker may represent a hundred or more franchisors. In the best networks, the broker is trained to help a prospective franchisee narrow their choices to a handful of opportunities for which they are well-suited.

When you first start working with a broker, chances are they will want to qualify you—both as to your capitalization and the speed of your decision-making process. They will then lead you through some of the same self-evaluation processes outlined in this book to narrow their list of franchisors to perhaps three to six—and will introduce you to all the names on your short list. At that point, they will pass you off to the salespeople for the franchise companies. While they will continue to follow up and get feedback (which they will share with the franchisors), their role in the sales process is largely over.

Typically, you will not pay a fee to the franchise broker. They provide this service in exchange for a success fee (essentially a commission) paid by the franchisor—typically in the range of $20,000 or more—if an introduction they make results in a sale.

In deciding whether to work with a broker, think in terms of the advantages and disadvantages. First consider the advantages:

- ✄ A broker will have a virtual warehouse of franchise opportunities. And since they will get paid regardless of which opportunity you choose, they can lend a degree of objectivity to your selection process.
- ✄ A well-educated and experienced broker can guide you through the process of self-evaluation better than you can on your own.

✄ Brokers will often know the back story behind many franchise companies and can help you evaluate risk vs. return.

✄ Because they know a great deal about the franchise universe, brokers could introduce you to franchise concepts that you might never have otherwise considered (but which may, nonetheless, be a great fit for you).

✄ The best broker networks will screen their franchisors before accepting them as clients. If a franchisor has a history of failed franchises, gets poor validation from its franchisees, has a large number of lawsuits against it, or simply does not yet have enough experience, it may not be accepted.

✄ You can work with a broker without paying anything out of pocket and walk away without penalty if things do not work out—much like working with a real estate broker.

Then think about the disadvantages:

✄ Since brokers may represent 100 to 200 franchisors, this will limit your choices to less than 10 percent of the franchise universe. If a great franchisor chooses not to use brokers, you may never hear about them. And, in some cases, brokers may screen out younger franchisors who do not yet meet their profile (but who might meet yours).

✄ While the best brokers will focus on you and your needs, some may have motivations that do not coincide with your best interests. Some franchisors may pay higher fees than others, for example. Others may offer broker spiffs ranging from bonuses to free vacations for top-referring brokers.

✄ Since a broker gets paid only if you buy a franchise (and, of course, one they represent), they are obviously motivated to push you toward buying a franchise—even if you are not a good fit for franchising.

I should emphasize that most brokers have a genuine concern for the franchise buyers who work with them. Ultimately, brokers are a great resource that can provide genuine value, but they are not the completely unbiased buyer's advocates some would have you believe. And even the most altruistic broker will be subconsciously influenced by the factors discussed above. So while brokers are a resource you should certainly consider, ultimately you should make certain they have steered you in the right direction.

If you would like more information on how to find quality brokers in your market, you can go to the iFranchise Group website (www. ifranchisegroup.com/brokernetworks).

Trade Shows and Industry Shows

Another great place to get information on franchises you might want to consider is at franchise trade shows and, if you are looking in a specific field, industry shows. Franchise shows in particular will give you an opportunity to speak with several hundred franchisors from a variety of industries in just a couple of days.

These shows have other advantages as well. Generally speaking, they offer seminars on all aspects of franchising—giving you a chance to learn before you buy. These seminars feature topics like industry trends, understanding contract provisions, veterans' franchise programs, financing, and overall success as a franchisee and are often worth attending. The shows also have vendor exhibitors who might help you as you move forward with your franchise investment, in areas such as finance, real estate, insurance, and franchise law.

Keep in mind that these shows may not provide a representative sample of the franchise marketplace. The exhibitors tend to skew slightly toward younger franchises and ones with lower investment levels.

A list of some of the better franchise shows and events is found in Appendix A.

Industry Associations and Other Sources

One of the other things you'll find at these trade shows is some great resources that can provide information and assistance in your journey toward business ownership. But whether or not you go to trade shows, you should definitely avail yourself of what these resources have to offer.

The International Franchise Association (IFA) is a good place to start. Their website (https://www.franchise.org/) contains a wealth of information on franchising. In addition to allowing you to search select franchisors, it provides information on industry suppliers in areas such as finance, insurance, veterans' programs, minority programs, and the franchise buying process. While the IFA tends to focus more on franchisors than prospective franchisees, it is a strong industry advocate and an organization you may eventually want to join.

Likewise, the U.S. SBA is a tremendous resource for aspiring business owners. At its website (https://www.sba.gov/), you will find a tremendous amount of information about SBA-guaranteed business loans and learn where to find an SBA lender in your local market. The SBA also offers access to business counselors who will assist you at no charge through programs such as SCORE, the Women's Business Center, the Veterans Business Outreach Center, and others. And with literally hundreds of SBA District Offices and Small Business Development Centers (SBDCs) providing free or low-cost counseling on everything from market research to financial assistance to business plan development, these resources are available to you almost anywhere. The SBA also has a number of educational courses that will further your knowledge about business ownership in general; these courses can be accessed online.

The SBA also publishes a list of SBA loan default rates by franchise concept. A simple search will turn up the names of the franchisors with the highest and lowest loan default rates. While a high default rate should not be a de facto deal killer, it should certainly raise a red flag when it comes to calculating their risk factor.

Reputation

Once you have narrowed the field to perhaps a dozen franchisors, one crucial screen you need to employ before making your short list is to understand the company's reputation in the marketplace. Spend some time searching the internet for general information on the remaining names on your list.

In doing so, do not just search for the companies by name. Search for the company name along with risk-related search terms like "default rate," "franchise failure," or "litigation." While much of this information will be included in the franchisor's FDD, these searches might lead you to details that will not be found in the FDD.

On the internet, of course, assessing reputations can be tricky. If you are looking at online blogs or other review sites, bear in mind that some posts (especially anonymous ones) can be factually incorrect or even posted by competitors trying to undermine a franchisor's position in the marketplace. While you will want to look into their claims, give these posts the weight they deserve based on their ability to present facts. And if you do find something of genuine concern, by all means raise the issue with the franchisor.

Visit the Competitors, Even If You're Not Buying!

Another thing you should be doing is visiting competing businesses—both franchises and independents—in your community. You may even want to talk to competing franchisors, even if you are not interested in them, so you can hear how they position themselves vs. your target franchise. If there are significant franchise competitors that have not yet entered your local market, you may want to do your homework on them as well, as they may end up being your competition in a few years, when the franchisor is ready to expand to your city.

Start by visiting any local establishments that are in the same general segment you are considering. Visit them at different times. If a business is likely to be busy on the weekends, go in during some off-peak hours. Talk to the staff, who are often surprisingly willing to share information about how the business is doing if approached correctly. Get a feel for how these businesses compete in the marketplace.

If you are interested in a business that does not have a physical presence, spend your "drive time" on the internet looking at their website. (Of course, you will want to do this even if they do have a physical location.) Note their prices and how they position the offer. Try to get a feel for how big their market is. If it is a service-based business, call them up and ask for a quote.

Remember, a franchisor could have the greatest concept in the world, but if the market is already saturated, you need to take that into account in your risk equation.

Find out what advantages they have and how they will compete with you. Ask them the same questions you asked your targeted franchisor. If you are conversational in your approach, they may answer some more detailed questions. What support services can they count on? What does their fee structure look like? What do they think of the market and the franchisor? Perhaps they can tell you something about the company that you didn't already know.

While you are at it, you may also want to visit locations for your target franchisor in some more distant markets. See whether they are all run in the same manner. Do they offer the same products and services, and at similar prices? Are their locations laid out the same? Are they all clean and well-run? If your first reaction is, "I can do a better job than they do," that is not a good sign. That means the franchisor may not be doing a good job of quality control—and those substandard franchisees will ultimately be representing you, as they will be flying the same flag and telling their customers what they can expect when they visit your location.

While you are at it, try to get a feel for what the owner or manager of the business does on a day-to-day basis. What may appear glamorous when reading about it on the internet may turn out to be more mundane when you are doing the job day in and day out.

This is one of those areas in which a lot of us fall into the love trap. We get our hearts set on a particular franchise and fail to see that there are already 50 similar franchises in our neighborhood— many of which may be struggling. Don't fool yourself into believing that it's a sign the market is strong. That will only reinforce your emotional decision.

Ultimately, every business must succeed at the local level. Drive around for a day or two, tool around on the internet, and start taking notes. Who are the competitors in the businesses you are considering? How long have they been around? What are their competitive strengths and weaknesses? What is their pricing structure? What kind of locations do they have? Write it all down—it will provide the grist for some good questions for prospective franchisors later on.

As a last step, you will probably want to contact a market analytics firm. These firms will, for a small fee, provide you with a market analysis of the demographics of the area and of the local competition. And some of these firms will indicate whether your market segment, at least in general terms, is overbuilt or underbuilt.

The better you know your market, your competitors, and your target franchisor's operations, the better equipped you will be to make an informed investment decision.

THE BOTTOM LINE: YOU CANNOT EXAMINE THE UNIVERSE

If you have been conscientiously screening your prospective franchisor candidates and doing your research, you should have narrowed your field of franchise candidates to a select few by now. Hopefully, you've eliminated any prospective franchises for which you are not suited temperamentally or for which you have no aptitude. You have gotten rid of any opportunities you cannot afford. And you've cut any industries you felt were too risky because of potential changes in the marketplace.

But if you still have dozens of prospective franchises that meet your criteria, you need to narrow the list further. To avoid "analysis paralysis," you need to get your list down to a handful of opportunities. So you will need to apply additional screens to reduce your list to a manageable number.

The screens you choose to employ are up to you, but they should focus on what is important to you in your decision-making process. For example, you could look at:

✂ the size of the franchisor,

✂ the age of the franchise system,

✂ the strength of the management team,

✄ the financial strength of the franchisor,

✄ the competitive nature of the market,

✄ or dozens of other potential factors.

In choosing your additional screens, be sure you understand how each one works. For example, one screen might be the length of time a franchisor has been in business. Franchisors who have been in business for some time have probably refined their operating systems and their franchisee support capabilities. On the other hand, these franchisors may have some disadvantages as well. They may be in mature markets and may be priced in accordance with the reduced risk associated with them. They may also not be as cutting-edge as a newer market entrant. Thus, if you choose to use this screen, you may be choosing to decrease risk at the expense of return. And there is nothing wrong with that, if that is how you are temperamentally inclined.

Another possible screen is that of size. Like franchisor age, size will have several advantages. First, it will bring with it certain economies of scale. If, for example, the franchises you are considering will be assisting you in purchasing (either through direct purchasing relationships or through negotiated discounts), the bigger the franchisor, the more negotiating strength the franchisor will have. Larger franchisors offer other economies of scale as well. They typically will have significantly better name recognition thanks to a larger advertising budget. The disadvantage to larger franchisors is much the same as it is for older franchisors: Less risk may come at the cost of a lower return.

Ideally, you can narrow your short list down to a handful of companies.

But if you haven't yet, don't worry. While you will certainly have your work cut out for you, the next step—analysis of the company itself—has plenty of opportunities for further whittling down your list.

Chapter 5

A DEEPER DIVE

I f you have followed the steps outlined in this book thus far, you now have a short list of companies, perhaps clustered in several industries, that you are planning to investigate further. Now the real work begins. In this chapter, you will learn how to interpret the information provided to you by the franchisors you have targeted and use it to narrow your list even further.

Take the First Step: The Initial Franchisor/Franchisee Interview

Once you let a franchisor know of your interest, in most cases, you will be subjecting yourself to their process. And many franchisors will judge your candidacy, at least in part, based on your ability to follow that process.

Typically, it begins with a call between you and the franchisor's development officer. On this call, the development officer will generally want to start by qualifying you. They will want to explore your ability to afford the franchise, find out what motivates you, learn a little about your skill sets, discuss your deadline for deciding, and in all likelihood set an agenda (often with a specific timeline) for your decision-making process. The purpose of that agenda is to keep the decision-making process moving forward while giving you and the franchisor a chance to decide whether you make a good match.

On that call, and in any interactions you have with your franchisor, be sure to answer honestly. If you understate your net worth, for example, you may find yourself disqualified. If you overstate it, you may be in for a disappointment several weeks further down the buying process. And since you will likely be interviewing multiple franchisors, you should take notes on what was said in each call, lest these conversations all begin to run together.

If you tell the salesperson you are looking to buy a franchise a year from now, she may well suggest you begin the sales process in nine months, when you are closer to deciding. She does not want to spend her time educating you about a territory that may be sold by the time you are ready to buy and would rather spend her time on prospects who are in buy mode. Remember, if she asks you if you will be ready to decide in 12 or 14 weeks (which is often the approximate timeline), you are only committing to make a decision—not what that decision will be.

After that call, typically the franchisor will send you some additional material on the concept. Often this will be a brochure or an e-brochure, perhaps a video, and a FAQ. Also included will be a confidential information request form (or CIRF, although some franchisors may just call it an application) that will provide the franchisor with more details on your qualifications. You can view a generic sample of a CIRF in Appendix C. The typical CIRF will ask for contact information, educational background, business experience, income, balance sheet information, banking information, and references; it will also ask you to provide a release so the company can complete a background check. Generally speaking, the franchisor will want you to fill out that form as a first step in the process and will schedule a second follow-up call after you agree to complete it.

While a skeptic might see this form as intrusive, it is an important step in the process. It is in the best interests of both you and the franchisor to ensure you are financially and experientially qualified to be a franchisee. And again, the franchisor sees your ability to follow this process as a test of how closely you will be able to follow its system of operations. You should fill out this form as accurately and completely as possible. The CIRF does not commit you to anything; it simply allows the process to move forward.

After you have completed the CIRF, the franchisor will typically schedule a series of steps in the sales process, which will help you educate yourself about the franchise. The best franchisors will encourage you to say no at any point in this process if you decide against investing in the franchise.

The first such step might be a call to review the completed CIRF together, to be sure the franchisor understands your answers. As part of that step, the franchisor may want to review the franchise offering in a little more detail with you, using the brochure or other information. Subsequent steps may involve answering questions about the franchise, providing you with a copy of the FDD and making a subsequent call to review that document, discussing your franchise territory, walking you through the process of getting financing, introducing you to various members of the franchisor's team, and ultimately inviting you to a face-to-face meeting at the franchisor's headquarters (which is often called Discovery Day). Generally, the franchisor will be asking you for a decision shortly after Discovery Day.

Depending on the length of your short list, remember you will be going through this process with several franchise companies at the same time. When you decide against a franchise, let their salesperson know and continue the process with your narrowed field.

At this point, the franchisor should be supplying you with additional material to help you make your decision. This comes in two general forms: marketing material and the FDD that the franchisor is required to provide under FTC Rule 436. Your next step will be to do a deeper dive on both.

Franchise Marketing Materials and Messaging

During the sales process, the franchisor should send you a variety of information about the nature of their business and the franchise offering itself. That material and messaging is designed to be fun, be eye-catching, and present the offering in the best possible light.

Most marketing materials, videos, and websites are designed to get you excited about the franchise without providing you too much specific information. These materials are written by people trying to put their best foot forward, but they must be consistent with any information provided in the FDD and must also, in certain states, pass muster with state regulators. So while it is advertising, it is probably also a relatively accurate depiction of the franchise business.

That said, they are usually designed to appeal more to your emotions than your intellect. Too many people get caught up in the glitz and glamour in a brochure or video. They look at the images and think, "This is what it will be like: happy customers, money changing hands, smiling faces." It can often give you a false impression of what the day-to-day operations of a business are like—so make a conscious effort to view it dispassionately.

In reading this material, you will probably notice that the promised support is very vague and discussions of what you can achieve financially are almost nonexistent. This is partly because these documents are often submitted to state regulatory authorities before they can be used in certain states and partly because the best franchise consultants and attorneys scour them to be sure they contain no promises that cannot be kept.

So what will you find when reviewing a franchisor's marketing materials? What should you look for? First and foremost, they reflect the value the franchisor places on professional marketing. If the franchisor provides a high-quality brochure, professional videos, and slick websites, it is probably marketing-oriented. And depending on the nature of the franchise, this marketing focus may be important. After all, if they can't sell to you, how will they help you sell to your customers? Conversely, if they give you a brochure that looks as if it was photocopied, along with a website that looks like it was designed by a 16-year-old with a credit card and a six-pack of Red Bull, it may mean that the franchisor places little emphasis on marketing—or it can't afford anything better.

They will also tell you about the franchisor's values. Read between the lines. What do they emphasize? The market and its growth? Or the leadership and services they offer? Do they discuss what differentiates the franchisor in the marketplace? If so, is that differentiation sustainable?

As an aside, one of the best uses of the franchise brochure is to help you convince those around you that you are making a good investment decision. As you move forward with your franchise buying process, there will be amateur (spouses) and professional (bankers) naysayers you will want to show the brochure to, to help them feel more comfortable about your decision.

So file the brochure away for the day you go for financing. If it's a nice piece, your banker will love it.

What to Look for in the Franchise Disclosure Document

At some point, the franchise company will need to give you their FDD. As we discussed earlier, the FDD was born out of a number of high-profile franchise failures, in which many franchisees lost their life's savings. Essentially, the FDD requirement is meant to protect prospective franchisees from unscrupulous franchisors.

The Franchise Rule (16 CFR Part 436) prescribes that the franchisor must disclose some very specific information to prospective buyers at least 14 calendar days before they sign the agreement or make a payment to the franchisor. The rule also states that you, as the prospective franchisee, must have been presented with a signature copy of the franchise agreement and any related contracts at least seven calendar days prior to execution (and that the franchisor cannot unilaterally and materially alter the terms after that date without restarting the seven-day clock).

Once the franchisor sends you the FDD, they should want to schedule an FDD review call with you shortly thereafter. The point of that call is to make sure you understand the nature of the offering while taking some of the fear factor out of a document that may have more than 100 pages of disclosures and contracts. You should absolutely allow the franchisor to take you through this review.

Regardless of whether you do this review call, you will want to undertake an independent and thorough analysis of the FDD. At first glance, an FDD can seem like a very intimidating document. But it really isn't. You can look at the FDD as having three main sections. Items 1-20 provide an overview of the company, the franchise opportunity, and a plain language summary of the business terms that define the relationship between the franchisor and its franchisees. Item 21 contains three years of audited financial statements for the franchisor entity. And Item 22 contains a copy of the franchise agreement (and likely a few exhibits), which is the actual legal contract that would be signed between you and the franchisor should you be awarded a franchise. Much of the detail in the franchise agreement is also in the FDD, so there is a lot of overlap between the two.

Remember that the FDD is not a marketing document. In fact, the FTC's drafting guidelines for the FDD prohibit a franchisor from including extraneous information. That's a good thing for a potential franchise buyer.

Because the decision to join a franchise system is such a major step for most people, I strongly urge anyone who is looking at a franchise opportunity to read the FDD very carefully, and to retain the services of an attorney who specializes in franchising to review it for them as well. If your brother-in-law is a top corporate attorney in your state but doesn't have extensive experience in franchising, he's not the right person to look over the FDD for you. If you don't know a qualified franchise attorney, you can search the Supplier section of the IFA's website (https://www.franchise.org/suppliers/attorneys)

for an attorney that works with franchisees. Spending a bit of money to have a qualified franchise attorney review the FDD and advise you will be well worth it.

Whether you're investigating a franchisor that sells women's fashion or hamburgers, every FDD discloses the same 23 items. As you review the FDD, Figure 5-1 highlights the 23 separate disclosure items:

Figure 5-1. **Disclosure Items**

Item Number	Title	Details
1	The Franchisor, its Predecessors and Affiliates	This item contains general information about the franchisor and its history. It also includes a basic description of the business model that is being franchised and what industry-specific regulations might exist that impact the way in which the business is operated.
2	Business Experience	Franchisors are required to list a brief five-year biography for any officers, directors, owners, or key employees that the franchisee will interact with.
3	Litigation	Item 3 lists any pending or concluded litigation involving the franchisor over the past ten years.
4	Bankruptcy	This item includes any bankruptcies over the past ten years for the franchisor or any affiliates, owners, or employees who have management responsibilities related to the sale of franchises or the support of franchisees.
5	Initial Franchise Fee	Item 5 describes the amount and payment conditions for the initial franchise fee and any other prepayments (e.g., inventory) that a franchisee must make to the franchisor before they begin operations.

Figure 5–1. **Disclosure Items**, continued

Item Number	Title	Details
6	Other Fees	Item 6 lists any other ongoing fees that a franchisee must pay to either the franchisor or an affiliate company.
7	Initial Investment	The table in Item 7 summarizes the anticipated low-end and high-end ranges for the likely investment a franchisee will need to make as they develop their franchise.
		If the franchisor offers multiple formats (e.g., strip-center stores and kiosks in malls) of their concept, there may be more than one table shown in Item 7.
8	Restrictions on Sources of Products and Services	Item 8 details where franchisees must purchase inventory and other materials from, whether the franchisor or its affiliates have an ownership interest in any supplier, and whether the franchisor or affiliates receive revenues from the sale of products to franchisees. Franchisors are also required to disclose the total dollar amount of rebates, markups, and other revenues from the sale of products to its franchisees in the prior year, and what percentage of the franchisor's total revenues that represents.
9	Franchisee's Obligations	Item 9 contains a table that indexes specific sections of the franchise agreement that address the obligations of the franchisee.
		To understand the detailed obligations of the franchisee, you'll need to review the sections referenced in the franchise agreement.

Figure 5–1. **Disclosure Items**, continued

Item Number	Title	Details
10	Financing	Some (but not most) franchisors provide financing directly to their franchisees. If financing is offered, details of that would be found in this item.
11	Franchisor's Obligations	Item 11 summarizes the obligations that the franchisor has to support its franchisees.
		Other than a detailed table outlining the franchisor's training programs, this item tends to be written at a very general level, with few details of the actual support provided.
12	Territory	Item 12 states whether the franchise business receives any territorial protection against other franchise or company-owned locations that may be developed. It also indicates what limits may exist in terms of your ability to service customers by type or based on where they live.
		If the franchisor mandates any minimum performance requirements (e.g., minimum sales volumes by year), those would also be detailed in Item 12.
13	Trademarks	Item 13 lists any trademarks the franchisor has secured for the brand.
14	Patents, Copyrights, and Proprietary Information	Item 14 lists details the legal rights that a franchisor has in any intellectual property that is material to the operation of a franchise. Often, this section will focus on common law copyrights and trade secrets in which the franchisor claims rights (generally focusing on the Franchise Operations Manual and perhaps proprietary computer software) along with the franchisee's obligations relative to confidentiality.

Figure 5–1. **Disclosure Items**, continued

Item Number	Title	Details
15	Obligation to Participate in the Actual Operation of the Franchise Business	Item 15 details any requirements in terms of your direct involvement in the franchise business. Some franchisors require the franchisee to be the day-to-day operator of the franchise, while others permit more passive ownership.
16	Restrictions on What the Franchisee May Sell	Item 16 indicates what goods or services you would be permitted to sell as a franchisee, as well as the franchisor's right to add or remove certain goods or services in the future.
17	Renewal, Termination, Transfer and Dispute Resolution	Item 17 details the length of a franchisee's initial franchise agreement term, its renewal rights, the conditions under which the business may be sold by the franchisee, and how disputes in the system will be handled.
18	Public Figures	If the franchisor uses any public figures (e.g., a pro athlete or actor) to promote, control, or manage the franchisor, they must be disclosed in Item 18. Public figures must also be disclosed if they are an investor in the franchisor company.
19	Financial Performance Representations	About 60 percent of franchisors elect to include historical financial performance information in Item 19. If a franchisor shares any information with you such as revenues, customer counts, gross margins, or profitability, that information *must* be in Item 19.

Figure 5–1. **Disclosure Items**, continued

Item Number	Title	Details
20	List of Outlets	Item 20 lists a three-year record of how many company-owned and franchise units have opened, closed, been transferred, been terminated, or ceased operation.
		It also lists the names, addresses, and telephone numbers of all current franchisees, as well as those who have left the system over the past five fiscal years.
21	Financial Statements	The franchisor is required to include audited financial statements for the franchisor entity over the past three years.
22	Contracts	Item 22 contains any agreements or contracts, including the franchise agreement, which you will be required to sign.
		Examples of other contracts may include a license agreement for technology owned by the franchisor, a sublease agreement that you may be required to sign if the franchisor holds the primary lease for your location, any personal guarantees that you and your shareholders must sign, and any financing documents if the franchisor is providing financing to its franchisees.
23	Receipt	When you receive the FDD, the franchisor will ask you to sign and return a receipt page, located in Item 23.

To really amp up your discovery process and do your due diligence when narrowing down your short list of potential franchises, you will want to harness the power of the FDD. It is the most revealing document in terms of comparing a franchisor's compatibility with your own list of goals and values. The FDD gives you a window into how a franchisor operates by revealing the major factors that affect its day-to-day operations and overall mission. In the next few sections, I'm going to discuss some of the key things to look for in the FDD.

At the top of that list is something you read about earlier: management.

The Greatest Concept Can (and Will) Be Screwed Up by Bad Management

Time and time again, I've seen it: a tremendous concept brought to its knees by bad management, while mediocre concepts with great management are making money by the bushel. Perhaps the single greatest influence on the success of any business is the quality of its management. Good management can weather almost any storm, but bad management can, and will, destroy even the greatest concept. This is something to keep in mind as you determine your own potential as a franchisee (which we discussed in Chapter 4), but it's also a vital barometer to check when you're reviewing potential franchises. If a franchisor's management isn't up to snuff, you'll know it when you dig into your discovery process.

As a franchisee, what are you buying? More than anything, you are buying the expertise and systems developed and refined by others: expertise in how to start and run a business, in marketing and operations, in evolving a brand to continually meet competition, in managing a team that will provide you with support, and in establishing and creating value for your brand. You are "buying" management!

In looking at the FDD, the first four items discuss the management of the franchise organization. These are very important but often overlooked, so read them closely.

Age and Business Type

First, these sections tell you how long the company has been around and how long it has been franchising. We already talked about the age of a franchisor and the potential increased risk that comes with a more youthful organization, so I won't rehash that information here. But check to see how many times the franchise organization has changed hands to get an idea of its stability. And read it closely enough to be sure you have a good idea of what the business actually involves.

Is the franchisor a manufacturer? If so, you need to look beyond the franchise to the product being sold. Invariably, when manufacturers go into franchising, it is not because they want to sell franchises. It is because they want to sell product. This also becomes apparent when you look at Item 8: Restrictions on Sources of Products and Services, as this section details required purchases through the franchisor and outlines whether it will allow you to buy through third-party suppliers. Item 8 also discloses the amount of revenue the franchisor or its affiliates derive from these sales.

Being a franchisee for a manufacturer is not necessarily bad. It may mean reduced royalties because manufacturers frequently make their profit on the products they sell you. And it often means the organization will have significant resources to devote to its franchise program. What's more, many manufacturers virtually give away a variety of services geared toward increasing your sales. But there are disadvantages, too. Swarovski, for example, can avoid franchise laws in the U.S. because its "licensees" only pay a wholesale price for inventory that they resell. All the training and support is provided without charge, and the company even gave (rather than sold) some proprietary construction items to their licensees. Likewise, quick lube franchisors owned by oil companies have been known to provide equipment to their franchisees in exchange for the long-term supply relationship.

Ask yourself if the product in question will be around as long as the term of your agreement. Will it be able to maintain its current market niche for that length of time? Will it be able to maintain its margins? Will it continue to enjoy the same levels of consumer demand? Finally, will the manufacturer compete with you through other channels of distribution in the future?

On the other hand, the franchisor may be (and often is) an organization set up exclusively to sell and service franchises, operating under a license to use the intellectual property of the corporate location or locations where the concept was developed and tested. In this case, the franchise company may look very thin from the standpoint of capitalization—especially if it is an emerging franchisor.

If the franchisor is not distributing products through the franchise system and its sole source of revenues comes through royalties, the amount of royalties it receives will largely dictate the level of support it can provide to its franchisees. For example, if you own a consumer services franchise and the average revenue per franchisee is only $250,000 per year, a 5 percent royalty will only generate $12,500 for the franchisor. When you factor in the franchisor's staff salaries, office overhead, travel costs, and other expenses, that doesn't leave much for support, particularly if the system is relatively small (perhaps fewer than 25 franchisees) and franchisees are located in multiple states, making travel efficiencies more difficult for the support team.

Meeting the Principals

Next, in Item 2, look at the business experience of the principals. In this section, the franchisor must disclose the backgrounds of all partners, officers, directors, or "other individuals who will have management responsibility relating to the sale or operation of franchises." Training and sales personnel and other relevant staff may be disclosed here as well. In larger franchise organizations, this will frequently be a long list, while in smaller organizations, it may be quite short. In either case, you should examine it closely.

First, look at the longevity of the managers. Have they been with the company for a while, or are they all relatively new? If they have all been there for at least a few years, that probably indicates stability—or, if the brand is not evolving to meet the marketplace, staleness. If they have been there two years or less, management is probably still making their imprint on the organization. Newer management could also be a warning sign that they may not know the organization very well.

Change, of course, can be good or bad, so it shouldn't necessarily put you off. If you think change is needed to revitalize the concept, this may be a positive sign. If, on the other hand, you feel the concept is currently working well, you may want to address the issue in your interview with the franchisor. In either event, you should try to assess the team's ability to effectively implement change.

The next thing you should look for, especially if management hasn't been with the company for long, is relevant industry experience. If it's a fast food franchisor, does the management team have experience in the fast food industry? If senior management is brought in from outside the industry, do they have the qualifications to succeed in this particular space?

Look for breadth of experience as well. Does the team have experience in all the functional areas necessary to support a franchisee? If you see there is no one with experience in real estate, and that is an integral part of the industry you are considering, be sure to ask the franchisor how they will compensate for that gap.

Often you will find a management team who all have some common experience. For example, one franchisor we worked with was run by a number of people who all hailed from KFC. This occurs with some frequency, as people who work together know each other's competencies, and will often band together to form a new organization. This is not necessarily bad, and in fact can have several benefits. Management has worked together previously, and thus knows one another's capabilities. Moreover, since this is presumably a hand-picked team, they probably tried to recruit only the best and brightest. So don't dismiss such teams out of hand.

Next, look for experience in franchising. Franchising is an entirely different animal from whatever industry you are considering. When a hamburger chain begins offering franchises, they are creating a new business that does not specialize in hamburgers. Their new business specializes in selling, and more importantly servicing, franchises. Ask if the management team has relevant franchise experience. How much? And was it with a highly regarded franchisor?

Look at the concentration of experience. Is the vast majority in the hands of one or two people? What happens if they get run over by a bus? Will the organization be suddenly bereft of expertise?

Examine management's history. Do they have a track record of building businesses and selling them off, or will they stick around for the long term? In general, the younger the franchisor, the shorter track record its management team will have. Again, this comes down to risk. To offset that higher risk, you should gain something you would not have with a larger franchisor. Perhaps it is a more cutting-edge concept. Perhaps it is a business you truly love or feel you would excel at operating. Perhaps it is your belief that the business model offers higher returns. A smaller or less-experienced management team doesn't mean you should cross that company off your list—it just means you need to evaluate how that increased risk is offset.

Before investigating further, put the FDD down and go back to your computer. While Item 2 in the FDD will tell you what each of these people has been doing for the past five years, it's a good idea to look beyond that. So conduct an internet search of the management principals by name. Check out their bios on LinkedIn or other business-oriented sites. Look for the same things we talked about above. Do they have a track record of success? Do they have the appropriate credentials? Have they jumped from job to job? How old are they? (While you could not ask that in a job interview, you are planning on investing your life's savings with these people, so you want to know if they are close to retirement age.)

Litigation

Ideally, the franchisor in question will not be involved in any litigation, past or present. But if it has been, in Item 3 it must disclose any current litigation or any litigation history, criminal or civil, in which it was convicted or held liable for the past ten years.

More important than the existence of litigation is the nature of any litigation in which it has been involved. Examine the litigation closely and ask yourself the following questions:

✄ What is being alleged in the litigation and by whom?
✄ Are most of the lawsuits being brought by franchisees? If so, can you envision yourself on the other end of a lawsuit one day?
✄ Does this litigation claim improper disclosures or inducements to buy?
✄ Does it allege fraud or unfair competition?
✄ Was there inadequate support or breach of contract?
✄ What was the disposition of any cases?
✄ Has new management been installed since the actions that were claimed in the lawsuits?

Just because a company is sued does not mean there is any merit in the claims. All too often, people sue hoping for a settlement. (Franchisors are reluctant to settle, of course, as it then becomes a tacit admission of culpability that they must disclose.) If the franchisor brought the lawsuit, a countersuit is a typical retaliatory tactic. If you see a lawsuit that concerns you, you should certainly investigate it further to see if it truly has merit.

If the suit involves a franchisee, you can always try calling them. While they are likely to be reluctant to talk to you about the lawsuit, as a franchisee of the system, they can certainly give you their opinion of the franchisor. Of course, there are two sides to every story. Make a note to ask the franchisor what happened as part of your due diligence, should you move to the next step with this company.

Another cause for concern would be if any pending lawsuit sought a judgment that would put a serious financial burden on the franchisor, endanger its intellectual property, or otherwise impair its ability to perform if it lost the suit. The concern, of course, would be that an adverse judgment might wipe out the franchise system.

To determine the level of risk, ask your attorney (more on that later) to give you an understanding of any adverse consequences. For example, you may want to look at the aggregate damages demanded in various lawsuits and compare that amount with the franchisor's capitalization. If the party adverse to the franchisor were to obtain those damages, would the franchisor survive the blow? (If you do not have a background in finance, ask your accountant that question as part of the financial modeling you will do in Chapter 7.)

One thing you should note is whether these lawsuits are brought by franchisees or by third parties. For example, some lawsuits may be brought by employees or customers of a franchisee but will name the franchisor simply because they have deeper pockets. The bigger the company, the bigger the target for many attorneys. These "vicarious liability" actions may say something about the degree of control the franchisor has attempted to exercise over its franchisees but say nothing about their relationship with or their support for their franchisees.

Another major concern would be a significant number of lawsuits—especially if they were initiated by franchisees. First, if your prospective franchisor is involved in that many lawsuits, it will be devoting substantial time and resources to legal fees—which, at a minimum, will mean it will have fewer resources to devote to its franchise network. More important, if the franchisor is involved in a great deal of litigation with its franchisees, that says one of two things about the franchisor: either it is inclined to resolve differences in court or it has developed a pattern of questionable behavior.

But again, it is not as simple as counting the cases in the FDD. Remember, what may appear to be a large number of complaints against a franchisor loses significance as the size of the franchisor increases. Ten lawsuits against a franchisor with 10,000 locations will matter much less than ten lawsuits against a small franchisor that has only been in business for a year. Likewise, the older the company, the more likely it is that disputes will have risen to the legal level. Older franchisors are sometimes operating under legacy contracts that are not as litigation-resistant as the ones developed by astute franchise attorneys today. You will need to exercise some judgment when calculating the risk associated with a franchisor's litigation history.

History of Bankruptcy

Finally, in Item 4 of the FDD, you will find information on the bankruptcy history of the franchisor and/or any of its principals or officers spanning the past ten years. This will give you valuable insight as to their management skills. At the same time, you should bear in mind that a bankruptcy in one's past is not an absolute indictment of a franchisor's ability to grow. After all, Henry Ford filed for bankruptcy—twice—before founding Ford Motors.

Bankruptcies can happen for a variety of reasons that are not necessarily an indicator of bad management: The death of a partner, a liability claim arising from an accident, divorce, job loss, medical expenses, or other unexpected turns of events might all fall into this category. In some cases, though, a bankruptcy (whether personal or corporate) can be attributed to poor financial management. If you see a history of bankruptcy, you will need to determine if the underlying cause could be poor financial management.

In the final analysis, evaluate the franchisor's management team with a critical eye and ask yourself if betting on them will increase or decrease your risk.

Fees and Services: If You Pay Peanuts, You May Get Monkeys

Potential issues with management should be at the top of your list when it comes to vetting a franchisor, which is why we discussed them in such detail in the previous section. And, while every item on the FDD is important, some may be more important to you than others. One of those big-ticket items is money: what you must put into the franchise and what you get in return. It would be wonderful if there were a simple calculation to figure out your cost benefit, but there just isn't. Unfortunately, because the FDD is such a complex document, many prospective franchisees try to simplify it, and nowhere is this more apparent than in the items dealing with fees and services (Items 5, 6, and 8).

Frequently, the prospective franchisee will focus on either the franchise fee or the royalty and compare it to the competitors'. At a quick glance, the lowest fee seems the most attractive. Unfortunately, that's the equivalent of going to a used-car lot and buying the cheapest car you can find.

It is a huge mistake to make your investment decision based on the initial franchise fee alone. While you want a franchise fee that is reasonable and competitive, it is only one component of your total investment. In most franchises, it represents a relatively small fraction of that investment.

For most franchisors, the initial fee is not a significant profit center. They have costs associated with marketing the franchise, franchise sales, legal documentation, training their franchisees, and providing them with initial support until they are up and operating— all of which is theoretically covered by the franchise fee. So while fees in the tens of thousands of dollars just to join the system may seem excessive, this is not where the franchisor makes its money.

Royalties should be much more important in your decision-making process. Let's say you choose to pay a royalty that is 1 percent higher than the fee of a comparable franchise offering. On sales of $500,000, that represents an additional $100,000 over the course of a 20-year agreement.

But shopping on the basis of royalty alone is not the answer, either. If you were to go to that same car lot and someone were to offer you a ten-year-old Chevy for $50,000, you would think they were crazy. But if they offered you a brand-new Ferrari for that same price, you would jump at it. The real question, then, is not price, but *value*.

At this point of your analysis, though, don't try to assess the value (we will do that later). Just have a good understanding of the fees you are likely to incur. In addition to the initial fee (found in Item 5), Item 6 of the FDD provides you with a table documenting all the fees the franchisor will collect from you. So if the franchisor has a 5 percent royalty and a 1 percent technology fee, you would pay a total of 6 percent. Go through this section closely to determine exactly what your commitments will be.

Also be sure you understand how these fees are actually calculated. For example, while most franchisors charge franchise fees based on gross sales, some charge royalties based on gross profit (revenues minus the cost of goods sold). Some franchisors may have different definitions of "gross sales"—for example, excluding taxes or gift card revenues.

The one set of fees you may want to view differently as part of this analysis are your advertising fees, referral fees, or national accounts charges. Unlike most other fees, these fees are geared toward driving revenue to your business. As such, you should view them as nonincremental (as presumably the franchisor has designed them); they will benefit you directly and are based on the franchisor's assessment of what has been historically necessary to drive business to your door.

As a side note, some franchisees have taken issue with the way a national advertising fund is spent; for example, it is often used to offset a portion of the salaries in the franchisor's marketing department. But those are expenses you would incur (either as incremental salaries or agency fees) if you had to conduct this advertising yourself. In fact, an internal marketing team may be less expensive than relying on one or more outside agencies.

This is also a good opportunity to take a look at Item 8 of the FDD, in which the franchisor must disclose any restrictions on the sources of products or services that will be imposed on you. Any franchisor that is looking to control quality will dictate the sources of any products or services that will impact the integrity of the brand— and that ultimately affects your costs, fees, and bottom line. Frankly, it is generally in the best interests of the entire network to ensure that the franchisor enforces these brand standards.

On occasion, the franchisor may be one of several suppliers or even the sole designated supplier of certain products and services. Many franchisors will choose to sell products and/or services to their franchisees. This will also be disclosed in Item 8, along with the revenue (not profits) that the franchisor or its affiliates derived from those purchases. Item 8 is also where the franchisor discloses any rebates or other incentives it receives from designated suppliers.

When the franchisor sells to you, it should have the opportunity to make a reasonable profit from those sales. In many systems, the profit a franchisor makes on product sales may allow it to reduce the fees it charges in other areas, such as royalties. Likewise, we have seen a number of franchisors who will redistribute manufacturer's rebates to their franchisees or who will contribute some or all of those rebates into their advertising fund for the benefit of all franchisees.

If the franchisee is acting as a captive channel of distribution for the franchisor, make a note of it here. Later in your diligence process, you can ask any franchisees you interview whether the franchisor's pricing is reasonable.

Estimating Your Investment

The next thing you will find in Item 7 of the franchisor's FDD is an estimate of the initial investment required to open a franchise. While you should already have a good idea of the general investment based on your prior research, at this step you should do a deeper dive to be sure you have a more granular understanding of the investment you will need to make.

One of the first things you will note is that investment ranges are sometimes very broad. And while the FTC has indicated that it wants to see narrow, meaningful ranges, it is unlikely that the broader ranges will change anytime soon.

One of the problems is that the franchisor must wear two hats when providing these estimates. While in his marketing hat, the franchisor wants to show a low initial investment, to encourage as many candidates as possible to apply. And while a good franchisor does not want to mislead a franchisee or attract franchisees that are undercapitalized, they may develop the low end of their estimate based on the best possible scenario.

The high end of the range is often developed while the franchisor is wearing his legal hat. The franchisor's lawyers will tell him he should cover the highest possible reasonable expenses so future franchisees cannot come back and sue based on the claim that the franchisor intentionally understated costs in an effort to mislead.

Another reason these numbers are sometimes inaccurate involves the base of knowledge upon which the franchisor draws to come up with the estimates in the first place. Especially with new franchisors, there is a danger that the estimates are fairly rough, perhaps coming from a limited number of observations in a small number of markets several years ago.

Finally, different franchisors may interpret the line items differently. For example, one of the typical line items is for "Additional Funds," representing the franchisee's working capital needs. The rule states that this number should be for a "reasonable initial period," which is defined as "at least three months or a reasonable period for the industry." You can see how one franchisor might opt for three months of working capital and another, perhaps in the same industry but with a different marketing program, might opt for six. Moreover, what constitutes these additional funds can be subject to interpretation. One franchisor might include a market salary for an owner-operator during the startup phase while another might not. Thus, what one franchisor interprets as necessary additional funds may be different from the next.

Of course, this is just one example. But it illustrates the point that in looking at Item 7, you need to dig deeper than simply taking the dollar amounts shown in the table at face value. Read the footnotes and be sure you understand the differences between any franchisors you are comparing for each line item listed. See the sidebar on page 98 for more information on the most typical Item 7 disclosure items.

Before moving on from Item 7, you can and should supplement the investment ranges provided by the franchisor with some additional research on a computer or over the phone. For example, you can:

TYPICAL ITEM 7 DISCLOSURE ITEMS

As you read the information in Item 7 of the FDD concerning your initial investment, you will typically find the following categories of investment items. In some cases, some of these line items may be eliminated, and in some franchises, other categories of investment may be included.

Bear in mind as you review these investment elements that they are almost always set up as a range of fees. At the low end, the franchisor will wear their marketing hat—trying to make the lowest reasonable estimate of what this might cost you. At the high end, the franchisor will wear their legal hat, trying to protect themselves from a claim that they underrepresented the size of the investment. The truth often (but not always) lies somewhere in the middle.

In examining the fees in Item 7, make sure you also read the footnotes to each of the investment lines, as they will include the assumptions used to derive the specific investment line items.

- ✂ *Initial franchise fee.* This is the one-time payment you will make to the franchisor upon execution of the franchise agreement.

- ✂ *Lease, utility, and security deposits.* For leased locations, the range typically includes deposits equal to first and last month's rent.

- ✂ *Design and architectural fees.* Any fees the franchisee will pay to a designer/architect.

- ✂ *Leasehold improvements.* Leasehold improvements include permanent construction items at the franchisee's facility, such as drywall, flooring, cabinets, countertops, HVAC, plumbing, electric, and other items that would remain should the franchisee leave.

- ✂ *Furniture and fixtures.* Furniture and fixtures include "nonpermanent" construction items, such as lighting fixtures, interior graphics, and display shelving.

- ✂ *Equipment.* Some franchisors may require you to purchase certain equipment you need to run your business. In some cases, you may need to purchase

TYPICAL ITEM 7 DISCLOSURE ITEMS, continued

vehicles (which might be broken out as a separate line item). Read the footnotes closely on this item, as the assumptions about how the equipment or vehicles are paid for or financed will be an important part of your investment decision.

✂ *Signage.* This includes both interior and exterior signs (although they may be broken out separately).

✂ *CRM/back office system.* This includes computer hardware and software for credit cards/gift cards, thermal printers, and business management software.

✂ *Other equipment.* This includes items such as laptops, telephones, smart boards, projectors, security systems, etc.

✂ *Professional fees.* Professional fees include fees paid by the franchisee to accountants, attorneys, and other advisors as they evaluate the franchise opportunity, negotiate the franchise agreement, and develop their business location.

✂ *Initial inventory.* The initial inventory includes the franchisee's first order of materials and general supplies for their location.

✂ *Insurance.* This typically consists of the first quarterly or semi-annual premium payment.

✂ *Business licenses and permits.* This item covers fees paid to governmental agencies.

✂ *Training expenses.* Such expenses typically include the cost of travel, meals, and lodging for the franchisee (and their manager, if appropriate) to attend the franchisor's training program.

✂ *Grand opening advertising.* Many franchise systems require franchisees to spend a specified minimum amount on grand opening advertising when their facility opens.

✂ *Additional funds.* This figure represents the amount of cash the franchisee should have on hand during the first three to six months of operation, to cover any cash-flow needs while the business is building a customer base.

> ✄ call local real estate agents to determine market rents for similar locations.

> ✄ speak to real estate agents, landlords, and tenants in comparable sites to determine the kind of tenant improvement allowances provided in the market.

> ✄ check job sites on the internet to determine prevailing wage rates for employees in your market.

> ✄ speak to insurance agents about the cost of business insurance.

> ✄ speak to franchisees (more on that later) about the costs they incurred, and, very importantly, how long it took them to get to cash-flow break-even.

As you review the Item 7 table, carefully read the footnotes. Many of the important details are found here. For example, most franchisors that focus on free-standing locations include a footnote that the cost of land is not included in their cost estimate—an important point if it turns out the land will cost the franchisee somewhere between $500,000 and $1 million. A footnote may also clarify whether the estimated cost of equipment or vehicles assumes they are purchased or leased. If you are purchasing the equipment outright, you will, of course, have a large upfront payment but no ongoing payments, whereas leased equipment will result in a lower initial investment and greater ongoing expenses—so this will be important when developing your cash flow model.

In evaluating a franchise opportunity, the ultimate test must be a financial one. Pinning down an estimate of your initial investment is one of the most important tasks in the risk-return analysis of your potential franchise investment.

Understanding Your Obligations

Item 9 in the FDD is presented as another table, this time outlining where you can expect to see any other obligations you will commit to as a franchisee. The FDD does not go into detail as to the nature of those obligations; instead, it cross-references any provisions in the franchise agreement where you can find them. This is another part of the agreement where it is particularly important to understand your commitments and their implications, so you will want to have the advice of legal counsel before making a commitment.

The obligations in this item are typically broken into the following categories, although some of them may not be applicable depending on the nature of the franchise business. They include:

a. Site selection and acquisition/lease
b. Pre-opening purchase/leases
c. Site development and other pre-opening requirements
d. Initial and ongoing training
e. Opening
f. Fees
g. Compliance with standards and policies/operating manual
h. Trademarks and proprietary information
i. Restrictions on products/services offered
j. Warranty and customer service requirements
k. Territorial development and sales quotas
l. Ongoing product/service purchases
m. Maintenance, appearance, and remodeling requirements
n. Insurance
o. Advertising
p. Indemnification
q. Owner's participation/management/staffing
r. Records and reports
s. Inspections and audits
t. Transfer
u. Renewal
v. Post-termination obligations
w. Noncompetition covenants
x. Dispute resolution
y. Other (describe)

While you will want your attorney to review these obligations with you in detail as you get closer to a decision, you should familiarize yourself with a few of them before going any further.

One area of particular interest at this stage is territorial development (e.g., mandating unit openings, the need to add salespeople, the need to add vehicles, etc.) and sales quotas. While some franchisors will have relatively limited or no territorial development or sales quotas, those that do may tie them to remedies (default, territorial reduction, etc.) that could significantly decrease the value of your franchise.

If you are considering passive ownership (where you would not work in the business full time but instead be an investor), you will certainly want to look at the section on owner's participation. You may find that the franchisor requires an owner to take part in day-to-day operations, in which case they are simply not a good match for you.

Most (but not all) franchise contracts offer some renewal provisions after the initial term of the contract expires. Once all your renewal provisions have been exhausted, the franchisor is under no obligation to renew your franchise. Of course, many franchisors will continue to renew their franchisees even then, but from an investment standpoint, you cannot count on that. Thus, in calculating your ROI, you will need to treat your franchise investment as one of limited duration.

You will certainly want to be sure you understand the initial term, post-termination obligations, and noncompetition covenants (preventing you from operating a similar business, either while you are operating the franchise or after you have left the system) you are agreeing to, especially if part of your growth plan involves the development of complementary businesses or the purchase of complementary franchises. Depending on how these clauses are worded, the franchise agreement may prevent that. McDonald's, for example, does not allow its franchisees to operate any businesses other than a McDonald's restaurant during the term of their contract, whereas there are numerous Burger King franchisees who also own Pizza Huts or KFCs. When you have a qualified franchise attorney review the FDD (see Chapter 8), she will be able to tell you if the noncompete provisions are in line with most other franchisors.

Again, the purpose here is to see if there are any nonstarters in this document. Be sure you review any areas that might conflict with your long-term goals. While these would certainly be uncovered later in your legal review with your attorney, you do not want to spend the time, capital, and emotional resources pursuing a relationship that is destined to never get off the ground.

Bigger Isn't Always Better

One of the most common mistakes both franchisors and franchisees make is the assumption that the bigger the territory, the better off the franchisee. Franchisees fight tooth and nail for bigger territories, and occasionally neophyte franchisors designate territories larger than necessary to "give the franchisees an edge."

Unfortunately, this reasoning is flawed at its core. Who, exactly, is locked out of a protected territory? The competition? No. A protected territory locks out members of your own chain. While franchisees from your system may ultimately compete with you for customers, those same franchisees are also contributing to a common advertising fund that promotes your location and drives customers to your business. The proliferation of these franchisees from your system will likely help you achieve greater buying power, thus reducing your expenses. In many instances, since your product offering will be similar and based on common marketing, you may be offering similar prices, so the customers you lose will be lost because of location—not because of a price war or product differentiation. And those fellow franchisees will, by sheer force of numbers, help position your brand as the dominant brand in a marketplace, making it more difficult for your franchisor's competitors to enter the market.

Now remember, we are talking about an agreement that may last 20 years or more. What will happen to the market in that time? Well, if it grows, perhaps your market will grow to support many more franchises. But if your franchisor granted a territory that is too big, who will grab that market share? Your competition, that's who.

Competitors may soon be opening all around you. And before you know it, you are out-advertised five to one, and revenue begins to decline. You are out-purchased five to one, and thus your selling price is higher relative to your competitors (or your margins are lower). You are out-locationed five to one and can't gain increased traffic from outlying locations. In short, too big a protected territory can negate many of the benefits of being part of a chain and may therefore hurt you from a long-term competitive standpoint.

The bottom line is that you will have competitors in your marketplace, whether you like it or not. And generally speaking, it is better if those competitors are part of your franchise, promoting a common brand, than part of another system.

So how big is big enough? Unfortunately, that's very difficult to judge, especially from outside the industry. Look at the territory being offered by the franchisor and compare it to the territory offered by direct competitors. That should give you a feeling of approximate scale. You can also make some estimates based on presumed market share. Look at a market of known size—say, approximately 100,000 people. If four of your franchisor's units are prospering in that market, you might assume that a population of 25,000 would support a unit. But if you looked at that same market and found that the largest competitor was prospering with ten units, you might judge that a territory of 10,000 would be adequate.

While it is not always necessary to go to this length, you should at least try to estimate based on the FDD how many units will eventually be placed in your market area. Remember, it's OK if it seems a little crowded.

While we're on the subject of territories, there are a couple of other things you should be aware of. First is the case where the franchisor does not offer an exclusive territory. Some franchisors, like McDonald's, no longer offer their franchisees an exclusive territory (or limit it to the specific street address). Companies such as McDonald's, however, take care to ensure that units are not located so close as to cause franchisees to lose a significant portion of sales. Other franchisors offering no exclusive territory, however, have seen numerous complaints on the issue of encroachment. Since there's no way to tell how much your franchisor will protect you by reading the

FDD, your best bet is to include some territorial questions when you interview franchisees later on.

A second, and often much more important, question about territories involves the specific rights granted to the franchisee. In the early 1980s, Häagen-Dazs, a new ice cream dipping store, was all the rage in the U.S. Owned by Pillsbury at the time, this franchise was dedicated to the sale of their proprietary ice cream through these stores. Many franchisees were having tremendous success. Then Pillsbury introduced products to be sold through supermarkets, and the war was on. Franchisees claimed that the franchisor, which had granted them protected territories, was unfairly competing with them and trading off the goodwill they had developed. Pillsbury, on the other hand, pointed to its contract, which gave franchisees exclusive rights to dipping stores within that territory but specifically reserved the rights to develop other channels of distribution.

When the dust (and lawsuits) settled, Pillsbury came out the winner. They were allowed to sell their products through supermarkets, but they had a flock of unhappy franchisees to deal with.

The lesson? Read the territory section thoroughly—especially if the franchisor is a manufacturer or currently operates through other channels of distribution. See what rights the franchisor is reserving for itself. Is it reserving the rights to distribute mail order catalogs in your territory? To distribute products to your competitors? To develop alternative channels of distribution? Will you get a cut if it does? Will you get preferential pricing? Some franchisors will reserve these rights even if they have no plans to exercise them, just to maintain flexibility. Try to picture a worst-case scenario to quantify your risk.

Term: How Long Is Long Enough?

Most franchise agreements are written for a specific term, often with renewal provisions that give the franchisee the right to renew the franchise agreement (often there are multiple options to renew).

Most franchise agreements are written with an endpoint to protect the franchisor if it elected to migrate away from a franchising strategy. One common question is, "What happens when the final term of the last franchise agreement expires?" For many franchise systems, this occurs 20 to 25 years from the date a franchisee joins the system. Technically, at that point the franchisor is under no obligation to extend your right to operate as a franchisee. However, as some legacy systems, such as McDonald's and KFC, reached that milestone, they elected to offer a new term to their franchisees. While franchisors will probably want to keep you in the system as long as you are performing, bear in mind that you cannot count on a longer term than is promised in the contract.

When looking at the term of agreement in the FDD disclosures, you need to concern yourself with only a couple of things. Since the franchisor will generally have the right to alter the terms of the agreement (such as royalties, advertising assessments, etc.) at the time of renewal (asking you to sign the "then current agreement" as a part of the renewal process), the initial term should be long enough to provide you with an adequate return on your investment (we will discuss this in more detail in Chapter 7).

Generally, the term of the agreement should also take into consideration the size of the investment you are making—the larger the investment, the longer the term. Including renewal provisions, you would usually expect a combined term of at least 20 years on average.

Second, the term should not pose any barriers for you relative to securing leases or financing. For example, the SBA will often want the initial term of the franchise contract to be at least as long as the term of the financing if it is going to extend financing to a franchisee. Landlords might similarly look for a term of at least seven years on some leases. Thus, if your franchisor offers a five-year term, you may find yourself in some negotiating difficulty with a lender or landlord.

Home Is Where the Heart Is

Another area of concern can sometimes be imputed (estimated to have a certain cash value) from the location of a franchisor's units and their stated plans for growth, as found in section 20 of the FDD. In this section, you can look to see if a franchisor's units are tightly clustered or scattered far and wide. If a large franchisor has numerous units, a wide dispersal shouldn't pose any problem, as they will probably have the support organization in place to deal with them.

However, if a smaller organization has units all over the country, it may mean the franchisor is expanding for the sake of expansion and is not concerned with pursuing a reasoned growth plan. When units are clustered, they can be more effectively serviced. Scattered units, however, require more travel time to visit and are more difficult to control. Moreover, they generally cannot capitalize as well on economies of scale (such as advertising and purchasing power) or on the synergistic effect that multiple units in a market will sometimes provide. This goes to the heart of the issue of management's business acumen and/or their apparent greed.

An exception to this rule is when a franchisor relies heavily on very specific site criteria for unit success. For example, if a concept is a one-per-city operation, a franchisor may need to focus on national expansion early on. So while McDonald's might have more than a hundred locations in Chicago, Hard Rock Café might open a single location and move on to the next market.

A second question you should ask is, "How close is the franchisor to my hometown or base of operations?" Again, with a larger franchisor, this may not matter as much, but if the franchisor is not close, and especially if there are not already a number of units in your area, you may receive less than stellar service. Ask the franchisor if they can provide the service you need.

Finally, look at the franchisor's proposed expansion strategy, also found in this section under "Projected Openings." Are they planning to grow so fast that they may have difficulty supporting their franchisees? Again, this is relative. For a large franchisor, opening 50 franchises in a year may be fairly simple. For a small one, 20 may be impossible.

Historical Performance

Finally, and perhaps most importantly, Item 10 also contains information on the number of transfers, closures, and failures over the past five years. Look at these numbers closely and determine what percentage of franchisees have gone out of business (to do this, divide the number that went out of business by the total number of franchises) to see how well the franchisor's system seems to be working.

Unfortunately, understanding these numbers so you can quantify your risk is not necessarily simple. Item 20 has multiple charts tracking things like "Transfers," "Terminations," "Nonrenewals," "Reacquired by Franchisor," and "Ceased Operations—Other Reasons" for franchisee operations. Interpreting this data is not always easy. Let's consider a couple of examples.

Transfers are exactly what they sound like. They occur when a franchisee transfers his business to a new franchisee. They can be a natural part of a franchisor's existence, or they can be a sign of problems. For example, if you were to invest $200,000 in a franchise, run it profitably for five years, and sell it to another franchisee for $500,000, that would be considered a transfer. Likewise, if you were to invest the same amount in the franchise, run it at a loss for five years, and sell it for $100,000, that would also be considered a transfer. As the franchise system ages, one would anticipate a higher number of transfers, as people begin to cash out or retire.

Terminations and nonrenewals can likewise be a good thing in some instances. While a termination may be terrible for the terminated franchisee, franchisors will sometimes do it with the health of the entire system in mind. Terminations can occur for numerous reasons. Sometimes a franchisee is not doing a good job of representing the brand (and not living up to the standards set in the operations manual). Perhaps the franchisee was convicted of a felony or went bankrupt. As a potential franchisee, you are left to interpret whether the number of terminations was a result of a franchisor doing some painful but necessary housecleaning, or if they were based on a different set of circumstances.

The category known as Reacquired by the Franchisor can likewise mean a few different things. Franchisors may choose to reacquire businesses from their franchisees rather than allowing them to fail. This can be both bad and good. On the one hand, it could indicate a failed franchisee who might otherwise be found in the "Ceased Operations" category. On the other, it says two things about the franchisor. First, they obviously believe in the viability of the reacquired franchise. And second, if your franchise were to fail, the franchisor might (but certainly would not have to) buy you out, even at a loss.

Of course, this category could have nothing to do with failed franchises. The franchisor may have simply exercised a right of first refusal (which most contracts contain) when the franchisee got an offer too good to pass up. Or a franchisee may have had a personal problem (death, divorce, etc.), and the franchisor bought the unit until it could be resold to another franchisee. Or the franchisor might have a strategic plan to focus corporate growth in certain markets. Again, you will need to interpret the numbers here.

Finally, the Ceased Operations column, while perhaps the easiest to understand, still leaves some room for interpretation. One would usually assume the franchise failed. But the franchisee may have died or simply lost their lease.

The age of the franchise system will affect your observations. For established franchisors, ask yourself how long the oldest franchisees have been in business. Has the concept worked in a variety of geographic markets and demographic settings? The older the franchise system, the more likely it is that you will see transfers, reacquired franchises, and perhaps franchises that ceased operations.

At the same time, if your franchisor is fairly new, you will not be able to properly assess this risk factor. For example, even though a franchisor may have opened a number of franchises over its first three years of operation, these locations may not yet have had time to fail. They may be limping along, eating through their capital reserves, in hope of turning the corner soon.

Item 20 also contains a list of contact information for past and current franchisees. Only by speaking with them can you obtain the background information necessary to interpret the tables in Item 20.

As you conduct your due diligence of the franchise system, you should call as many current and former franchisees as you can (more on this later). They are free to provide their opinions on the franchise opportunity, the quality of support they receive from the franchisor, what challenges exist in running the business, what it takes to operate the business successfully, and how they have performed financially. Talking to them is one of the most critical aspects of evaluating any franchise opportunity.

Where There's Smoke, There's . . .

While there are several other potential problems to look for when examining the FDD, many of them rarely appear.

One such problem would be whether, in reading Item 13 on Trademarks, you were to find that the franchisor's trademark was not registered or was under dispute. The name is of vital importance to you as a franchisee, so such disputes should raise serious concerns.

Another issue would be if the franchisor relied heavily on public figures to promote or support the franchise (found in Item 18, Public Figures). The danger is that the death of that public figure or their fall from popularity might severely hamstring your business.

Other things may jump out at you as well. The franchisor may have termination clauses that you deem unreasonable. It may have onerous transfer provisions that make it difficult to sell your business. It may make you sign other agreements you feel are unreasonable.

So go through the FDD and its attachments closely and eliminate any franchisors that give off a bad odor.

The Franchise Agreement

One of the required disclosures in the FDD is a copy of any contract you may sign, including the franchise agreement. While the disclosure rules require the FDD to be drafted in plain English, there is no such rule regarding the contract.

While the franchise agreement may give you some insight into the relationship not found in the FDD, unless you are an attorney (and probably even if you are), you need to be sure your attorney reads this document and advises you as to your rights and obligations prior to signing it.

And make no mistake, the contract is not stacked in your favor. Partly because of current franchising law and partly out of necessity, franchise contracts are often presented on a take-it-or-leave-it basis to buyers who have never purchased a business before and who often do not know the right questions to ask.

As a management consultant who helps franchisors structure the business terms in these contracts, I can tell you firsthand that franchisees and franchisors do not enjoy a level playing field. Every franchise contract I have ever seen is stacked strongly in favor of the franchisor.

Never *Trust a Statistic*

You've heard the old saying "There are three kinds of lies: lies, damned lies, and statistics." Not only is it true, but perhaps nowhere can the results be more damaging than in franchising.

One of the most common statistical lies is the citation of franchising "industry" statistics. Statistics that reference the success rate of franchisees in general as a means of implying that your chances of success are similar can be a major source of confusion. Twenty years ago, it was not uncommon to read something like this: "According to the U.S. Department of Commerce, nine out of ten new businesses will fail in their first ten years. But only 4 percent of franchisees go out of business in any given year."

Read that quickly, and you might think, *Hey, this franchising sounds like a sure thing.* Which is, of course, exactly what the franchisor wants you to think. But let's look at the statement more closely.

First of all, a close reading reveals it is comparing two different statistics. Whenever this happens, *beware!* If 4 percent of franchisees go out of business in any given year, how many go out of business in 10 years? Depending on how you do the math, it would be somewhere between 33.5 percent and 40 percent.

So franchisees would have a success rate of 60 percent or better, right? Wrong! Because we are also comparing two different statistical groups—*new* businesses vs. *all* franchisees, including those that have been in business for years and presumably have a lower failure rate. Look closely to see if a statistic is comparing apples and oranges!

But even if the same groups were being compared, the most insidious statistic is the one that is hidden the best. This is the problem found in grouping franchisees into an "industry." Franchising is a means of expanding a business, not an industry. While franchisees may be more likely to succeed due to the systems and support services they receive, that has *absolutely no relevance to your likelihood of success*. When you consider a franchise system, the franchisor can provide you information on the longevity of its franchisees. Ask them what percentage of their franchisees still owned their businesses after five, seven, or ten years. What percentage of their franchisees have closed since they began franchising? For franchisees who have sold their businesses, what is the average length of time they are in the system before they sell?

Of course, this is just one example. But you need to examine each part of the franchisor's message closely to be sure you understand precisely what is being stated, what is being implied, and what is left unsaid. Focus on the actual claims being made and note how they are worded to get at the truth behind the statistics.

THE BOTTOM LINE: THE MORE HOMEWORK, THE BETTER

As you evaluate a franchise system, I recommend you also compare the information in their FDD with those of their primary franchise competitors. How do they compare in terms of:

✂ the depth and experience of their management team?

✂ the franchisor's experience in operating company-owned locations?

✂ the size and geography of their franchise system?

✂ the fees they charge?

✂ the support they provide?

✂ the performance numbers disclosed in Item 19 relative to the size of their investment? (If the financial performance is marginally lower but the investment is half that of a competitor, the ROI might be much greater even though unit-level revenues are lower.)

✂ the failure and turnover rates of their franchisees?

While some of this information can be obtained by visiting competitors' websites or looking at online franchise portals such as Entrepreneur's Franchise Hub (https://www.entrepreneur.com/franchises), there are a number of sources from which you can obtain FDDs. If the franchisors you're looking for are registered in California, Minnesota, or Wisconsin, you can find their FDDs on the state government websites at no cost. You can also purchase most FDDs from third-party sources such as www.franchisedisclosures.com, FRANdata (http://www.frandata.com/), The FDD Store (https://www.thefddstore.com/), the FDD Exchange (https://fddexchange.com/), and other websites you can easily find via a Google search.

You should also run a Dun & Bradstreet (D&B) report on your franchisor. D&B reports provide financial and payment information on both public and private companies. Your banker will probably be willing to run it for you at no charge, and you may be very happy he did—especially if you find that, contrary to what you saw in the franchisor's financial statements, the company is not as financially healthy as it seems.

Visit actual sites in your market or region. Don't tell the franchisor that you plan to do it; just drop by to see what's happening there. (We'll talk more about interviewing the franchisees later.) Watch to see how busy the operation is and how well-run it looks (and whether it appears to run in a manner that is consistent with others you have seen).

With this information in hand, you are ready to do a little more one-on-one research. It's time to talk with the franchisor.

Chapter 6

MEETING THE FRANCHISOR

I f you have done your due diligence thus far, you've probably already interacted with someone from the potential franchisor's team—perhaps the person in charge of sales, marketing, or business development. Chances are that is how you received the FDD and other important documents you've used to review the franchise. From this point on, you will need to interact regularly with the franchise salesperson (and probably other members of the franchisor's team), either over the phone or in person.

Your best strategy when dealing with franchisors on your short list is to treat the process as a collaboration in which you both stand to gain financially if the deal goes through. Both you and your franchisor should be trying to learn more about each other in a kind of business courtship that will ultimately lead to a long-term relationship. At least for now, you are on an equal footing.

In this chapter, you will learn about the intricacies of meeting franchisors in person. First, you should be aware of a few minefields that potential franchisees may encounter during the sales process.

The "Award" of a Franchise

The best franchisors "award" franchises. They are serious about their commitment to quality, and only the best franchise candidates will qualify. Unfortunately, the worst franchisors hide behind the word and use it as a sales tool.

Once you start your franchise search, you will almost certainly hear that a franchisor organization will award a limited number of franchises in your territory. The word connotes a highly selective process in which a franchise territory is granted to the winner of a long line of prospective candidates. In fact, the best franchisors take selecting a franchisee very seriously. They recognize that the success of their organization is founded on the bedrock of franchisee success. In fact, they realize that the single most important factor in the success of any franchise system is the strength of the franchisees that are brought into the system. Successful franchisees earn more (and pay more royalties). They require less support and often invest in additional franchise locations. They do not litigate. And they validate well with new candidates in the franchise system.

While the best franchisors are truly selective in their franchise sales process, somewhere along the line less selective franchisors hijacked the jargon, using words like "award" to create a sense of urgency in their buyers. Instead of using it as a formula for success, they just use it to help close the sale. If they do their job right, you will be so tied up trying to win the approval of the franchise selection committee that you may rush unwisely into an investment. Thus one of the most important rules of the franchise sales process is: "Always remember—they're salespeople."

Today, a typical franchise development officer (aka franchise salesperson) with a seven- to ten-year track record of success makes a base salary of $85,000 to $100,000, plus a commission of perhaps

$5,000 per sale. Good franchise salespeople can easily double their base salary every year on commissions. This can easily motivate overzealous sales tactics.

Of course, there are some companies that really do believe in the concept of awarding a franchise. Pretzel retailer Auntie Anne's launched its franchise program in the 1990s and awarded about 650 franchises in the first decade. To discourage overeager salespeople, the company compensated its development staff on straight salary and did not pay commissions. Other companies have incorporated the franchisee's long-term performance into the salesperson's compensation. But most companies, and most salespeople, are still largely commission-oriented.

Franchise salespeople are paid to present a franchise opportunity in the best lights, so you need to be careful that you are not the victim of a particularly skillful salesperson. Choose the franchise *you* want—not the franchise someone else wants you to buy.

Trust, But Verify

The vast majority of franchise development officers, despite their financial motivations to sell, are honest and reputable. They do not want to sell you a franchise that will fail, since that's also bad for the franchisor they work for. And, truth be told, when it comes to those few disreputable franchise salespeople, the honest majority of franchise salespeople are among their loudest critics. After all, the salespeople who play fast and loose with the rules hurt everyone's reputation—and they can take sales away from franchises where the prospect might really be a good fit.

As a franchise buyer, it's sometimes difficult to discern the sales-driven organizations from those that are truly selective. While most are honest, it is imperative that you protect yourself from those who care only for their commissions—not your success.

Please do not take this as a license to be adversarial in the sales process. One of the things a good franchisor is trying to ascertain is how well you get along with their team—and people in general. If you treat your franchise salesperson like a used-car dealer, you will likely be shown the door.

That said, caution is vital to a successful negotiation, so be on the lookout for anything that seems strange in the sales process. Specifically, here are some red flags that should make you very concerned:

- ✂ Telling you something that is inconsistent with the franchisor's FDD. The more inconsistent it is, the more likely it is that the alteration was deliberate.

- ✂ Implying you will do better financially than the numbers in the FDD. This might be by saying that your investment will be at the low end of the range in Item 7 or your revenues or margins will be at the high end of the range in Item 19 (more on both of these in Chapter 7). Or they might provide you numbers that are better than the range (or give you numbers where none were listed in Item 19). There may, of course, be legitimate reasons they might expect you to generate better numbers (a newly designed prototype operation or a market in which the franchisor already has a strong presence, for example), but if they cannot explain why you will do better (or, even better, show you a subset of numbers demonstrating why you should expect improved performance), you should exercise a great deal of caution.

- ✂ Implying that you *will* or *should* achieve the median numbers (or any numbers, for that matter) in the franchisor's FPR in Item 19. The financial performance in Item 19, which is almost always strictly historical, is not supposed to be a projection (although you will want to use it to create your own projections later).

- ✂ Steering you to talk to particular franchisees as you go through your validation process. If there is a good reason to speak to those franchisees (they are all in your chosen market, they are operating a new prototype, they all started in the past two years), that might be reasonable. Otherwise, exercise caution against speaking solely with cherry-picked franchisees.

✀ Any high-pressure tactics designed to get you to close should be viewed with a healthy degree of skepticism. Implying that a fee structure may be changing soon or that a territory may soon be sold to someone else (even if true) is designed to rush your decision. You may be better served spending more time on your due diligence.

✀ Watch out for an overabundance of "puffery." Puffery in the sales process often involves the use of unprovable superlatives and opinions rather than objective facts. If your franchisor claims to provide "the best support" or have "the happiest franchisees," those claims are impossible to refute. These statements are harmless as long as you recognize that they are essentially meaningless. But an overreliance on this sales tactic may indicate that the franchisor has nothing more meaningful to sell.

✀ How evasive is the franchisor when answering your questions? Judge this carefully. While your first reaction might be to perceive evasiveness as deceptive, it may just be that the franchisor is constrained by laws and/or best practices as to how they can answer the question you are asking. If a franchisor is avoiding your question, ask yourself if there might be a legitimate reason for the indirect answer you are receiving.

If you find yourself confronted by these tactics, an alarm should go off in your head, but don't stop your investigation. This might just be a new salesperson who has not been properly trained, or the franchisor may not know how the franchise is being represented. But the more prevalent these tactics are within the organization, the more likely this is an institutional characteristic.

Remember, as a franchisee, you are only as good as the franchise system you belong to. If you join a system that employs high-pressure salespeople, it is likely they have recruited a number of franchisees who are not well-qualified.

Underqualified candidates are more likely to fail. A lack of capital may cause them to take shortcuts relative to brand standards, causing quality at the consumer level to suffer. Failed franchisees are more likely to sue, which can cause the franchisor to go under—or at a minimum force the franchisor to spend money to defend this litigation, thus depleting resources that could otherwise be used for franchisee support. Poor validation from these franchisees will make it more difficult for the franchisor to grow in the future.

So if you feel you are dealing with a high-pressure franchise salesperson who has stepped over the line of "truth stretching" into pure fabrication, run for the hills.

Also be wary of franchisors who try a bit too hard to impress you. Maybe they send a limousine to pick you up at the airport or take you to dinner at an expensive restaurant. They may pay for your airfare to attend Discovery Day. They wear $1,200 suits and flash their Rolex as they pull out their Mont Blanc pen to sign the contract. While there is nothing wrong with this per se, check that they don't have their other hand in your pocket.

If a franchisor uses these tactics, they are doing it to impress you and get you to buy the franchise. But these fancy frills are meaningless as far as your ultimate success is concerned. The message should be clear. Someone has to pay for that limo ride and that expensive dinner. And the franchisor is hoping that someone will be *you*.

Perhaps they are trying to be gracious or demonstrate their level of professionalism, or perhaps they want you to think you are dealing with the best in the business and can always expect first-class service. But don't let these surface details keep you from looking beyond the show to the substance of the business opportunity and the long-term relationship you will have with the franchisor.

Until you know for sure, keep your hand on your wallet when you ride in their limo.

Meeting the Team

While some franchisors may wait until Discovery Day to introduce you to the team that will be providing you support, many offer you a chance to meet and interview them while you go through preliminary due diligence. The sooner you can speak to some of these people, the better, so you should avail yourself of this opportunity as soon as possible.

First, though, be sure you understand their roles and responsibilities (ask your development officer) and who they report to in the organization. That should tell you something about organizational alignment and priorities while giving you an opportunity to prepare specific questions for these meetings.

Of course, you will want to know how each of these people will provide support—either directly or indirectly—to you as a franchisee. But beyond that, you will want to understand how you will fit with the franchisor's mission and culture. Unlike your franchise development officer, whom you may see little of after you sign the contract, you may be entering into a relationship with some of these people that will last for decades—so be sure you like them, or at least can communicate well with them.

Remember, too, that with better franchise systems these interviews are also about qualifying you as a franchisee. Often, these people will be asked for their opinion about your candidacy and your fit within the organization. So while you want to get your questions answered, you also want to be sure that you interview well.

Discovery Day

The ultimate goal of everything the franchisor has done so far—the marketing brochures, the ads, the trade shows, the follow-up calls—is to get you to a face-to-face meeting, which in franchising is often called Discovery Day. This meeting, which almost always takes place at the franchisor's headquarters, is designed to sell you on why you should become a franchisee, and, at least with good franchisors, is also designed to be sure you are a good fit for the franchisor in terms of knowledge, experience, attitude, and culture.

So how does it usually work?

You are typically invited to fly or drive in for this meeting. Most of the time, you are responsible for your own travel expenses. Typically, you are asked to bring your spouse, life partner, or potential business partners with you—and you should absolutely do so regardless, as you will need their support not only to make the final decision but as you move forward with your business.

While there are many variations as to how Discovery Days are conducted and the order in which things happen, they generally have the following elements:

- ✀ Often, the franchise development officer meets you at the airport or at your hotel the night before. You may go out to dinner with the development officer and other members of the management team, so they (and you) can get a feel for how well you will mesh with the organization.

- ✀ The following morning (or when you arrive), you are often given a tour of the franchisor's headquarters and introduced to various people who will provide support to you as a franchisee. If you have not yet spoken to some of these people on the phone, you will probably interview with them at some point during your visit.

- ✀ As part of that process, you may have detailed meetings with the department heads who will be supporting you. These individuals may also demonstrate some of this support (the IT person showing how information is captured and key performance indicators are provided, the real estate person detailing how sites are analyzed, etc.).

- ✀ If the franchise has physical locations, you typically visit one or more nearby operating locations. During those visits, you may have the opportunity to learn in greater detail how the business runs and what your role might look like.

- ✀ The franchisor likely does a presentation on the company (often with PowerPoint slides) that will provide you with more background and an opportunity to ask questions.

- ✀ If you have not yet reviewed the FDD with your development officer, you go through it item by item and are asked if you have any questions about the contents. The franchisor uses this opportunity to sell you on making an investment in the franchise and to explain any warts you may have found.

✖ You may have additional discussions about how you intend to finance and run your business.

✖ You may be asked to take a personality profiling test (if you have not done this previously; more on this later in the chapter).

✖ You should have an opportunity to get answers to any final questions you may have.

At the end of the process, you are told that the award committee will review your information and make a final decision on your candidacy soon. Often you are told that the franchisor will be considering your application and will be given a timeline for the next steps. You may be asked for a tentative commitment, assuming the franchisor is willing to move forward with your candidacy.

To prepare for Discovery Day, the franchisor should provide you with a detailed agenda of the visit in advance. Once you receive that, you should develop a list of goals and questions you'd like to address during the visit. The more prepared you are walking into Discovery Day, the more you will get out of it.

Some of the questions you may want to consider asking your franchisor are listed on the worksheet in Figure 6–1 on page 124, but you should add more specific questions based on what you have read in their FDD and depending on the nature of your franchise opportunity.

Many of the most revealing questions you should ask your franchisor will be based on a thorough reading of the FDD. If the franchisor is involved in litigation, ask about it. If the franchisor has a significant number of franchise failures, ask about them. If the franchisor has been involved in a bankruptcy—ask.

Beyond that, other questions may occur to you based on your knowledge of the franchisor, the market, and the competition. You will need to come up with more specific questions, depending on your personal and financial situation, as well as the particular franchisor you're interested in.

Figure 6-1. **Questions for the Franchisor**

Listed below are some sample questions you should ask a potential franchisor. These questions are intended as a starting point for your analysis—so do not look at them as a complete list.

1. Tell me about your competitors, especially those operating in my local market. How will we address them based on your market analysis? _____

    _____

    _____

2. What kind of changes are on the horizon for this concept? Marketing? Operations?

    _____

    _____

3. How are you planning to respond to the competitive threat posed by current competitors? Potential competitors?

    _____

    _____

4. What is the biggest competitive threat in the marketplace? What is the biggest opportunity? (*Note*. Pay close attention here. If you don't get a substantive answer, either you are being sold or you are dealing with someone who simply does not know the answer. In either case, be wary.) _____

    _____

    _____

5. Who is your customer at the end user level? What is happening to this market?

    _____

    _____

Figure 6–1. **Questions for the Franchisor**, continued

6. What are you really selling? (For example, on one level, McDonald's is selling hamburgers. But on another, it is selling quality, service, and value delivered fast with a clean restroom.) _____

    _____

    _____

7. What has happened to the market over the past five years? To your market share? To your strategy? What new competitors have surfaced, and why? _____

    _____

    _____

8. Who are your major vendors? Do they give terms on initial inventory? What terms? What terms do they provide on ongoing purchases? _____

    _____

    _____

9. What are you doing to secure the best prices on products? Are you also negotiating with service and equipment vendors (e.g., insurance, office equipment, etc.)?

    _____

    _____

10. How much do you spend on research and development? How much as a percent of revenues? _____

    _____

    _____

11. What are you trying to accomplish with your advertising? Who is your agency? Why did you choose them? _____

    _____

    _____

Figure 6–1. **Questions for the Franchisor**, continued

12. Are there any plans to sell the business in the next five years? _____

_____

_____

13. Where do you see the company five years from now? Are you planning any major strategic changes in the concept? Do the owners plan on eventually selling the company or passing it on to their heirs? _____

_____

_____

14. What major changes has the CEO implemented since he took over (or in the past three years)? Is this part of an overall strategy? _____

_____

_____

15. How are you attempting to differentiate yourself in the franchise marketplace?

_____

_____

16. Are any major changes to management planned? _____

_____

_____

17. What support do you provide to franchisees that helps them build revenues during their first 6-12 months of operation? _____

_____

_____

Figure 6-1. **Questions for the Franchisor**, continued

18. In what ways do you collect best practices and share them with franchisees in your system? _____

_____

_____

19. What key performance indicators (KPIs) do you share with franchisees? In what way is the information shared? _____

_____

_____

20. Why are you not using an FPR (assuming they aren't)? _____

_____

_____

21. Joe Franchisee told me _____. How do you respond to that? _____

_____

_____

22. What is your biggest franchise disaster? Why did it occur? What has been done to prevent a reoccurrence? What is the name of the franchisee involved?

_____

_____

23. What is the best thing you can say about each of your competitors? What are their strengths and weaknesses? _____

_____

_____

Discovery Day vs. Decision Day

While it is not common practice, some franchisors have replaced Discovery Day with the term "Decision Day," and they will try to use the site visit to close the sale. They will have the agreements at least seven days before your visit so you can sign. They may even preface the meeting with something like, "If we are able to answer all your questions to your satisfaction, will you be ready to sign at the end of our time together?"

Franchisors figure (correctly) that by getting you to commit to a visit to their home office, you have deepened your psychological investment in the franchise and are thus more likely to buy (much like automotive dealers do when they get you to take a test drive). In fact, I heard one franchisor speak about this at an industry event some years ago; his advice was to be sure to have franchise prospects "bring their checkbook so you can sell them while they are still in the ether."

A Discovery Day positioned as a Decision Day is another red flag. You should be able to walk away from Discovery Day and process the information you've received. You should feel free to follow up with the franchisor's team on any additional questions that may have arisen during the visit. You should never feel pressured to make a life-changing decision on the spot.

These meetings can be very exciting. And with the pressure of the salespeople and an expectation of signing, it is all too easy to get caught up in the moment. Don't let that happen.

Choreographed Site Visits

If the franchise involves a physical location, the franchisor will probably suggest that you visit a nearby location to show you what their current prototype looks like, provide you more detail on how it operates, and help you better understand the role you will play on a day-to-day basis.

Look at this as a first date: for a date, you would dress up and look your best, and for this visit the franchisor will show you its best unit operating at its busiest time. If it's a restaurant franchisor, for instance, expect that you will go around the lunch or dinner hour, for example. The unit will be swarmed with people, all of whom will be happily buying the product you may one day sell. It will be hectic. As often as not, the unit manager will be so swamped she won't be able to talk. And you may think (as the franchisor wants you to), *What a gold mine!*

While there's nothing wrong with dressing up for a date, maintain your healthy skepticism. I was once asked to be an expert witness in a case (I declined) in which the franchisor would pass out coupons for free food redeemable on Discovery Days. Needless to say, the franchisees subjected to this trickery were not happy when the long lines they saw at units never materialized at their own locations.

So when you visit operating units, keep an open mind. If the location(s) you visit are owned and operated by the franchisor, pay particular attention to the standards they are maintaining. Take note of the following:

- ✂ Is the location clean and well-maintained?
- ✂ Does the quality of the staff seem high?
- ✂ How well do they engage with customers?
- ✂ How well do they engage with you if they are introduced during the visit?

If the franchisor doesn't do a great job in all these areas in the locations they operate near their home office, that is cause for concern.

The Office Tour

If you are visiting a larger franchise company on Discovery Day, chances are they will give you an opportunity to walk through their offices and meet their people where they work. If your franchisor has a manufacturing facility, prepare to don a hard hat as well. While you may not think so at first, the facility tour is of vital interest to you in making your franchise decision. Do not take it lightly.

As a franchisee, what you are buying is, in effect, the expertise of the people you are meeting and the culture you are observing. So ask questions. Ask to see samples of what they will be doing for you. If they are in advertising, ask to see samples of recent promotional campaigns. If they are in real estate, ask to see site packages.

Also get to know the people a little better. Ask them how long they have been with the company. If it has not been long, ask them what they were doing before. Observe what they have in their offices and how organized they seem to be. Even how they dress and how they interact with you will offer clues on their values.

It is important that you develop a personal rapport with the franchisor. After all, you will be working closely with this company—perhaps for the next 20 years or more. From that standpoint, it is not important to establish a good working relationship with the franchise salesperson—as they will, in all likelihood, be long gone before you have finished your first decade with the franchisor (or, if they are still around, will have minimal interaction with you unless you invest in another franchise). You should, however, feel the franchisor exercised good judgment in hiring and training the salesperson.

If you meet any of the equity owners of the franchise company, it is very important that you get along well and can establish a comfort level with each other. If you have a chance to speak with them, ask them about their goals for the company. Where do they see the company five years from now? Are they planning any major strategic changes? Do they plan on selling the company or passing it on to their heirs?

Ask questions about the competition and market trends. This is perhaps one of the most important, and yet most overlooked, areas in which you should gather data. How are they planning to respond to the threat posed by current competitors? Potential competitors? Where do they see the market going? And what competitive responses do they anticipate?

Listen closely to the way they talk about the competition. Are they analytical and forthright, or are they disparaging? There's an old saying: "Never wrestle with a pig. You both get dirty, and the pig likes it." If they are unprofessional in this regard, perhaps you should ask yourself why they feel they need to compete in that way. And, more important, whether you really want to associate with people who behave in a less-than-professional manner.

Another approach you might take is to interview some of the franchisor's staff who were not at Discovery Day. One key person who may not be at the Discovery Day meeting is the field business consultant (or similar title), who would be your main day-to-day contact in your market once you open. If the franchisor hasn't already suggested you speak with him, you should request an interview by phone or in person (assuming he lives close to you). Since you would likely interact with him more closely than with anyone else on the franchisor's team, it's important that you feel comfortable with him and feel he has the experience and skill level to be a valuable support resource. The field business consultant likely supports between 20 and 30 franchisees in your region. When you talk to existing franchisees in the system, I highly recommend you ask them how well the field business consultant performs, and how much value he brings to helping franchisees build successful businesses.

You might also ask to talk to people on the franchisor's marketing, training, or operations teams. Ask them what they like about the brand and what they like or don't like about working for the franchisor.

The bottom line is that you need to feel comfortable with your franchisor, their culture, and the team they have assembled. You've got a long road to travel together.

Be Sure You Know What's Being Tested

At some point during Discovery Day, you may be asked to take a personality profiling test. For years, I have been skeptical about these tests. I have seen successful franchisees come from all different walks of life, and the most successful appeared to have little in common. Most were hard workers and were willing to follow the system, but I didn't need an elaborate profiling test to tell me that. Recently, though, I have started to feel more comfortable with these tests, though I do not always encourage their use, as it is fairly easy for people to game the system.

I learned this almost by accident when I spoke to a franchise salesperson who swore by psychological testing—but not for the reason you might think. He told me the tests didn't mean much to him as far as potential success was concerned, but they did tell him everything he needed to know about *how to sell the franchise!* In essence, he was using these tests to have his prospective franchisees identify their own hot buttons. Prospects were telling the franchisor how they wanted to be sold!

Over the years, however, I've spoken with a number of franchisors who use profiling tools successfully as part of their franchise recruitment process. When used properly, they help a franchisor better understand the potential strengths and weaknesses of their candidates as business owners and members of a franchise system. Profiling tools are most relevant for franchise systems where the franchisee will be actively involved in day-to-day operations. They can help the franchisor (and the candidate, if the information is shared with them) identify the franchisee's tendency toward attention to detail, leadership skills, work ethic, and other factors that could be a predictor of business success.

If you're asked to take a profiling test, I recommend you agree to it as long as the franchisor is willing to share the results with you.

My personal ambivalence aside, I know a number of companies that swear by them. One such company, i9 Sports, has on occasion eliminated candidates from contention based on test results alone. And they feel strongly that it has made them a better franchisor. Some of the best management recruiters, including Peter Capodice at Capodice & Associates, have used them with great success. The research conducted by Greg Nathan of the Franchise Relationships Institute in Australia, and the profiling process he's developed specific to franchising, is considered by many to be groundbreaking. Many of the consultants at the iFranchise Group swear by these tests.

So if you are asked to take a test, take it and answer it fairly. But know that while most franchisors are probably using them for legitimate purposes, at least some franchisors and franchise salespeople are using them for an edge in the sales process.

Be Careful of the Meeting at a Hotel

Occasionally, you will run into a franchisor that wants to get together for Discovery Day in your hometown—maybe at a hotel or an airport lounge. While this tends to be the exception in franchising, if your franchisor offers, by all means take them up on it. This gives you an opportunity to get to know the franchisor without investing additional time or money in travel.

Just don't substitute this meeting for the trip to the franchisor's home office. You absolutely must visit the franchisor's office and meet their team before you make the final decision. Do not let the convenience of a local visit or any high-pressure sales tactic dissuade you. And if the franchisor hasn't already encouraged this visit, that should be a concern.

There can be reasons a prospective franchisor might not want you to visit them on their turf. Perhaps business isn't great, and they have just gone through a major layoff. Perhaps they have very little in the way of a support team to show at the moment.

Again, this is not an indictment of smaller or newer franchisors. Newer franchisors bring some significant advantages to the table. With a new franchise you will likely have the opportunity to work with the founder of the company instead of someone with significantly less experience. The franchisor, if they are smart, will place extra emphasis on your success, as the success of early franchisees will dictate the long-term success of the franchisor. You will be able to pick the best territories—and add territories before others join the system. And, as the company grows, early franchisees will often have the best seat at the table when it comes to providing input to the franchisor and the founder.

The point is not that you should only pick organizations with big teams. It's simply that you need to know what you are buying. So be sure you kick the tires—in person—before committing to anything.

The Group Interview

At some point during Discovery Day, you will likely have a group meeting with people from the franchisor's leadership team. These staff members will represent most of the departments you'll interact with as you develop and operate your franchise.

If you received a detailed agenda before Discovery Day, it hopefully included a list of the people you'd be meeting with. With that in hand, I recommend you develop a list of questions to address with the people who are responsible for specific areas such as site location, facility design, construction, training, marketing, finance, and general franchise operations. If you bring that list into the meeting with you, you'll be prepared to pose the right questions to the right people.

The group meeting may begin with the franchisor's team going through a structured presentation of the franchise opportunity and the support you'd receive as a franchisee. It often covers things like:

- ✄ market,
- ✄ concept,
- ✄ competitive positioning,
- ✄ franchise organization,
- ✄ support provided to you as a franchisee, and
- ✄ the process of moving forward with the franchise, should you choose to do so.

This is a fairly common approach. If you've not seen that presentation before, ask for a copy before you leave so you can review it later or share it with your advisors.

Following the presentation, you'll likely have a chance to probe deeper with the staff members in attendance. This is where your preparation will benefit you. Don't be afraid to ask questions. This is your best opportunity to speak with the people within the franchisor organization who would ultimately support you as a franchise owner.

Remember, this interview is a two-way street, as both parties are sizing each other up for success. Either at this meeting or throughout the day, expect they will ask you a number of questions to further qualify you for the franchise. Since they probably already know a lot about you from the time they have spent with you on the phone, the questions will likely be geared toward getting to know you better. And if you brought your spouse or significant other, they will want to involve them in the conversation as well. They may ask you where you see yourself in five years' time. Do you plan to open additional locations? What gives you the greatest satisfaction? What is your greatest accomplishment? How would you respond in [X situation]?

The goal here is twofold. The best franchisors want to be sure you are a good fit for the organization. But they also want you to feel as if you are interviewing for a position you may not get. In some circles, it's called the "negative sell"—making you sell the franchisor on yourself, rather than the other way around. Psychologically speaking, if they can make you feel as if you are competing for something, you are much more likely to want it.

At some point, you will probably be asked where you are in the decision-making process. They will want to cover what steps you have taken in areas like investigating your market and obtaining financing. And they may want to walk you through the FDD one more time to answer any remaining questions and uncover any lingering objections you may have.

I have provided a list of questions you should ask any potential franchisors in Figure 6–1 on page 124. You don't have to ask all these questions at Discovery Day. Some may be appropriate during the site visit. Others perhaps would be better when the salesperson is going through the FDD. And still others may be best during a follow-up phone call. But ask them. All of them. And any others you can think of.

Toward the end of the interview process, the franchise salesperson will want to get a preliminary commitment from you. That will often come in the form of a question, such as, "If you are approved by the committee, when do you think you'll be ready to move forward?" You may be told that the franchisor's application committee will be considering your application over the next several days and will provide some preliminary feedback on your candidacy. Keep in mind this preliminary commitment is just that—preliminary. You are not signing on the dotted line just yet. And, as opposed to the hard-sell Decision Day tactics you read about earlier, this is meant to gauge your level of commitment—not make you commit on the spot.

The franchisor won't be done with you once your in-person visit is over. With most better franchise organizations, there will be a debriefing after Discovery Day, where the people who met you will provide their input on how well you would do as a franchisee. In some organizations, a single "no" vote may be enough to jeopardize your candidacy, but in most, the business owner weighs their input and ultimately makes the decision.

Some old-school franchise salespeople may, at this point, use the application committee as an opportunity to play good cop, bad cop. By claiming to feel positive about you and your application, the salesperson (the good cop) can urge you to move fast before the bad cop (the committee) gives away your territory to another franchisee. The committee is faceless, so it gives you no one specific to dislike. It also represents a higher authority whose demands you supposedly must strive to meet. Rest assured, however, that whenever pressure is applied, it will come from the committee.

These tactics, for the most part, went out of favor about the same time as the horse and buggy, but if you encounter them, do not let them push you into a hasty or unwise decision.

Evaluate Information Sharing within the Franchise System

An important issue to address during Discovery Day is how well best practices are gathered and disseminated throughout the franchise system. Owning any business is a challenge, but a franchise system can lessen that challenge—if the franchisor has established good systems for collecting and sharing best practices among franchisees. The strength of the system is defined by the collective knowledge of the franchisee community. If you as a franchise owner lack access to that knowledge, the franchisor's value proposition diminishes substantially.

In a high-functioning franchise system, the franchisor gathers franchisees' financial data and shares the results through a web-based benchmarking platform. A franchisee should be able to log into that platform and see how her business compares to other franchisees by geography, age in the system, revenue volume, etc. There should also be a technology hub where franchisees can access best practices in marketing, sales, employee retention, and other key factors that help each franchise location succeed.

In your group meeting with the franchisor's team, ask them what systems they've put in place to gather and share this information. Also ask whether they share their company-owned data with franchisees. If they operate corporate locations, they should share that information as well.

Cool Off

After a long, grueling Discovery Day, you're finally on your way home. But you can't relax yet. You now have the information you need to decide—or at least most of it. But you still have work to do. Your first order of business should be to document your meeting. Since you will likely be meeting with multiple franchisors, you will need to keep track of all these details. While it does not need to be lengthy, you should probably note:

- ✄ Who was present
- ✄ When and where the meeting took place
- ✄ What levels of support were discussed
- ✄ What promises or commitments were made by either party
- ✄ Any information that will help you develop your financial model

In the process of documenting these conversations, you will likely come up with additional questions you will want to jot down for your next call with your development officer.

Finally, let the glow wear off. Look at some other opportunities or just take a weekend off from your search.

A cooling-off period isn't just a good idea in the abstract; it can protect you as well. When the Franchise Rule was originally adopted, the regulators built in a cooling-off period to prevent fast-talking salespeople from closing unsophisticated prospects before they had finished their search. Twenty years ago, it was not uncommon to present the FDD (which was then called the Uniform Franchise Offering Circular, or UFOC) at Discovery Day, sending prospects home with detailed written information after this initial meeting. Today, with the advent of electronic disclosure, you will almost always have received the FDD prior to your visit. And if there are no changes to the franchise agreement, the 14-day clock may have already expired by the time you arrive.

Don't Just Kick the Tires; Take It for a Spin

Finally, try putting yourself in the role of a franchisee for a week or so and see how well the "job" suits you.

In fact, some franchisors (McDonald's and Domino's among them) require you to work in a franchise or corporate location before being awarded a franchise. Sort of like SEAL training for franchisees, this trial run is as much about giving their franchisees a chance to ring the bell as it is about the franchisor wanting to see whether they can hack it.

Of course, most franchisors do not have this built into their sales process. But that doesn't mean you can't put yourself through your own version of SEAL training. Perhaps you can get a job working for a franchisee. Maybe you can't take the time to do this, or maybe there are no units close to where you live. But if you want to get a good feel for what you are getting into, you might want to ask your franchisor if they will let you try before you buy.

If you feel you have a particularly strong rapport with a franchisee in your area, perhaps (with the franchisor's permission) you could offer to work for a week or two for free. The franchisee gets free labor, and you get some insight as to whether you are cut out for the role.

Some franchisors may frown on this practice, perhaps fearing you are trying to obtain their intellectual property in order to compete with them. If this is the case, you might instead find ways to simulate their work environment. For example, you might spend some time at competing sites: Get there when they open and stay as long as you can every morning. In your calls with franchisees, spend time talking about what a typical day in their life is like. And talk to independents and competitors as well. Paint yourself into the picture.

Be sure you know what you are getting yourself into. A janitorial service franchise might sound like a great, low-cost business opportunity. But it may also mean you will be working late nights and sleeping during your children's baseball games. A bar and grill might sound like great fun, until you realize you will be open every day of the year and away from your family on most holidays.

THE BOTTOM LINE: UNDERSTAND WHAT YOU WILL DO, AND WITH WHOM

At this point, your research should have given you a great deal of background on the franchises you are considering. Hopefully, you also have enough insight to determine whether the business is a good fit for you.

You have ideally found one (or perhaps several) business that is well-suited to your talents and that you believe you would enjoy. Likewise, you have assessed the risk associated with the venture and are comfortable you can manage it. And finally, if you have gotten this far with one or more franchisors, you believe the team they have assembled and the system they have created will work.

But before signing on the dotted line, there is still more work to do.

The acid test for your final decision must include an examination of your projected financial performance and an analysis of whether the return you anticipate from your hard work and your investment will be worth the risk you will incur.

Chapter 7

HOW MUCH CAN I MAKE?

If everything is going as planned, you should now have a short list of opportunities you are seriously considering. All these opportunities should be acceptable to you personally, with franchise companies you believe will prosper. And all should have management teams you are willing to bank on.

Still, we have not answered the most important question: What can I earn?

Obviously, the main reason most people buy franchises is to earn money, but no good franchisor would ever answer that question directly. They would have far too much liability if they did. A franchisor should instead provide you with some guidance as to how you can estimate that performance for yourself, which starts with something we mentioned in Chapter 2: the financial performance representation, or FPR.

Analyzing the FPR

The franchisor's best tool for helping you understand your potential earnings is the FPR, which is found in Item 19 of the FDD. Almost always, the FPR focuses on historical results that have been achieved by the franchisor, its affiliates, its franchisees, or some combination of the three. The FPR may come in the form of an income statement, but more often, it will focus on some of the key variables that will dictate income (and will allow you to develop a pro forma income statement based on those variables). The format and utility of these FPRs vary from franchisor to franchisor.

Franchisors are *not* required to provide their franchisees with an FPR. In the early days of franchising, the use of an FPR (then called an earnings claim) was more the exception than the rule. In fact, in the late 1980s and early 1990s, less than 20 percent of franchisors provided one. Many were reluctant to share this data out of fear that it would result in litigation and were often warned against it by their lawyers. But over the past few decades, there has been a strong reversal of opinion on FPRs; by most estimates, the majority of franchisors provide at least some information in Item 19. In a 2018 study that looked at 1,497 FDDs, Rob Bond, president of the World Franchising Network, found that 61 percent included some kind of FPR.

Why No FPR?

Sometimes, the franchisor may not have an FPR. Its absence will make it difficult for you to estimate your revenues and profits. And while the uncertainty of your projections will increase your risk, that does not necessarily mean you should immediately eliminate the franchise opportunity from consideration.

Here are some of the reasons (good and bad) franchisors might choose not to provide an FPR:

✂ The franchisor may believe the units it could use for an FPR are, for some reason, not typical of what a franchisee might expect to make. In fact, it may believe its own performance will be stronger than the performance of the franchisee and may have avoided the FPR in order to be more conservative. For example, perhaps the franchisor has a unique location or has been in business for decades serving one community where the brand has become iconic. Perhaps the franchisor is franchising only part of its current operation, based on the belief that the franchisee needs to start with a less complicated business (perhaps evolving later to a fuller line of products and/or services).

✄ The franchisor may believe it will incur greater legal exposure by making an FPR (although this is probably not true, assuming the franchisor uses historical financial information as the basis for the FPR). But there are still some attorneys who feel FPRs can increase a franchisor's legal exposure. (As an aside, we believe the opposite is true. A well-crafted FPR should decrease the franchisor's exposure, as it helps the franchisor combat claims that its sales team made representations outside the FDD.)

✄ The franchisor may not want to disclose unit-level financial information out of fear that its competitors could use that information to their advantage.

✄ The franchisor (especially newer franchisors that have conducted most transactions at the unit level in cash) may historically have been understating its sales to the IRS to reduce its taxes, and now it cannot substantiate its actual levels of sales based on its own historical numbers.

✄ A new franchisor may not have an adequate operating history on which to base an FPR. For example, its locations may have been open less than a full year.

✄ The franchisor may have recently opened a new prototype that will be the basis for the franchise program, but it does not want to provide that information for fear of liability (e.g., a franchisee claiming that if he had known about the non-prototypical sales performance, he would not have invested).

✂ The franchisor may fear that its historical financial performance does not compare favorably with its competitors.

Obviously, those last few reasons should be of some concern to you as a prospective franchisee, and you should add those questions to your list for further discussion with the franchisor if it does not provide an FPR.

But regardless of whether the franchisor supplies an FPR, your next job must be to develop an estimate of what you can expect to earn as a franchisee. This is your most important task before purchasing any franchise.

Use, But Never Rely Exclusively on, an FPR

In doing your research, nothing should make you happier than finding out that a franchisor has provided an FPR. Generally that means it thinks it has something to brag about from a financial perspective. Moreover, it is making your job easier by telling you upfront what kind of financial results some of the units in their system are achieving.

If a franchisor supplies an FPR, you should definitely use it as a starting point. Most FPRs will provide you with great information, but you (and your accountant) should read them very carefully to be sure you understand how to use them in your business planning.

But as we said in Chapter 5, "There are three kinds of lies: lies, damned lies, and statistics." For example, there was one well-known franchisor that for years provided an FPR based exclusively on the performance of a handful of corporate locations. Those locations had far greater revenues and profits than the vast majority of franchisees in the system. But unless you read the footnotes closely, you might never know they were not a representative sample. While this kind of statistical juggling is no longer allowed under the new FPR rules, there are other methods (grouping by age, type of location, etc.) that could be used to give you unrealistic expectations (intentional or not).

Your first job, then, is to read the FPR thoroughly. Generally, it will have a load of disclaimers and footnotes. These are often as important as the financials themselves, so pay close attention. If, for example, the financials are based only on locations open longer than three years, you may want to ask yourself what the first two years looked like. If labor costs are reported, check whether those calculations include management as well as staff. So do some digging. And if you are not good with numbers, now is the time to get your accountant involved. (Even if you are good with numbers, you will still want them to look at your projections. More on that later.)

Also remember that no government agency has done any real due diligence on the document you are reading. While regulators in those states that require franchisors to register or file their legal documents prior to offering franchises for sale will have read the FPR to be sure it conforms to the rules regarding how the information is presented, they generally will not have checked the accuracy of the numbers. It is up to you to be sure you are getting reliable information.

As you are reviewing the information in the FPR, note the format the franchisor uses to present the information. Franchisors in the same industry may present very similar information in slightly different formats—so carefully note those differences. As you may have noticed, there are hundreds of different ways in which earnings information can be presented. (A good compendium illustrating this variety of FPRs can be found at https://www.freeitem19s.com/.)

Some franchisors include historical income statements—perhaps modified to incorporate line items for advertising fees, royalties, and other fees you may incur as a franchisee. These may be the best types of FPRs, as they allow you to compare the numbers you think you can earn with those that were historically achieved by the franchisor— but don't rely on them too heavily in your planning, as your market conditions may be different.

Other franchisors are somewhat less forthcoming with their numbers. Some may choose to only disclose sales numbers. Some may limit it to average selling prices, average sales per square foot, average sales per salesperson, or any of a variety of other indicators. Fitness clubs may be broken out by number of members. Automotive franchises may focus on the number of vehicles serviced per day.

Restaurants may show food and labor costs but not occupancy (as this is often best determined on a market-by-market basis). Hotels often include occupancy rates in their FPRs to enable you to project revenue based on the size of your facility.

Note: If a franchisor does use a historical FPR, you can ask to see "written substantiation for the financial performance representation" and the franchisor must provide it. So if you are not clear how the numbers were derived, ask.

Don't Do Anything Till You've Crunched the Numbers

Regardless of whether the franchisor supplies an FPR, you *must* develop a pro forma statement of cash flows (which basically predicts how much revenue will come in and the expenses incurred during a given period so you can understand your cash requirements and your profitability over time) for the franchise opportunity you are considering. In doing this, you should exclude some items you would normally find on an income statement, like depreciation, amortization, interest, and taxes, leaving you with a bottom line typically referred to as EBITDA (earnings before interest, taxes, depreciation, and amortization).

Let's break down the elements of EBITDA and why they are excluded. Depreciation and amortization are noncash entries that (other than reducing your taxes) will not impact your cash flow. We omit taxes from our analysis because most of your alternative investments are subject to tax in any event—so this allows us to better compare apples to apples. And we do not want to look at interest or debt service, as those numbers are a result of your deciding how to finance your business, not a function of which franchise you purchase.

This being said, your accountant may point out ways in which you can use a business to shelter otherwise taxable income. (Business necessities like the corporate Mercedes might fall into this category.) Finding these legal loopholes is worth the cost of hiring an accountant in the long run. Unless you have a background in finance and accounting, you should get your accountant involved early. And even if you do, you will want to have an accountant review your work before you finalize your decision.

As a first step, you should derive cash-flow estimates for a "mature" franchise—one that is at least two to three years old. This will allow you to measure the long-term returns offered by the franchise, as many businesses (especially in the service sector) are not very profitable (if at all) in their first year or two of operations. Of course, you will have to estimate first-year cash flows separately when calculating your required investment to be sure you have adequate working capital.

Once you have these numbers, you will have a good idea of what you can expect to earn from your franchise. So let's start crunching numbers. (Really. It's not that bad.)

Deriving Numbers When There Is No FPR

When the franchisor does not provide you with an FPR, you will need to get creative to accurately estimate the revenue your business can earn. There are several different methods you can employ, and you should try *all* of them.

A WORD OF CAUTION

In virtually every business plan I have ever read, there is a tendency to overestimate sales and underestimate expenses. This can be disastrous!

When franchise prospects make projections, they often gravitate toward the numbers achieved by the top performers in the system on the assumption that they are smarter, will work harder, and will work longer than the average franchisees. And while that might be true, I can assure you no one ever bought a franchise believing they would be on the lower half of the performance curve. Yet, by definition, half of all franchisees are.

Be conservative, and always remember Murphy's Law. Estimate low on revenues and high on expenses, and any surprises you receive will be happy ones.

Each method will result in a different figure. When making your final estimate, you should lean toward the methods that gave you the lower numbers, for the sake of being conservative.

Let's look at some of these methods.

Ask Someone Who Owns One

This is perhaps the most important step in this book. If the franchisor has existing franchisees, you should speak to as many of them as you reasonably can.

Every FDD must provide a list of current franchisees in the system, along with their names, addresses, and phone numbers. You'll find this information in Item 20 of the FDD. It must also disclose contact information for franchisees who have been "terminated, canceled, not renewed, or otherwise voluntarily or involuntarily ceased to do business under the franchise agreement during the most recently completed fiscal year." Call them!

Be sure you contact a large enough sample to give you a good cross section of results. For example, speak to newer franchisees as well as those who are better established. Talk to franchisees who are located fairly close or in your targeted geographic market. Talk to happy franchisees (current ones, presumably) and unhappy franchisees (those involved in litigation or who have been terminated, for

---

THE SECRET PASSWORD

Some franchisors instruct franchisees not to answer blind inquiries from prospective franchisees. From a franchisor's point of view, this makes sense, as competitors could find out valuable information about unit-level operations under this guise. But once you have had your initial meeting with the franchisor, there should be no problem with you contacting as many franchisees as you like. The franchisor may have to call them in advance, or it may provide you with a secret password that will let them know you are a legitimate candidate. But the franchisor should be happy to do so. If it tries to keep you from contacting franchisees, that should be treated as a major red flag.

example). Speak to franchisees who are operating in a similar type of location (strip mall, street front, etc.). And as much as you can, target franchisees with a similar background (for example, if you have no industry-specific experience). The franchisor may be willing to provide you with enough background information to identify some of these people. From a statistical point of view, you will get the most reliable information if you keep your sample random and your sample size is larger—but do work in these subsets.

If you are speaking to a franchisee who failed, you will certainly want to know why, and they are equally certain to give a bad reference when asked about the franchise. You will have to decide whether their opinions have merit and whether you can envision yourself on their side of the fence someday. You will definitely need to take some of what they say with a grain of salt. I have never found a failed franchisee who attributed that failure to his lack of intelligence or hard work, although clearly some do fail through their own fault alone.

Of course, no business can ever guarantee success, even if a franchisee is a good fit. But a large number of failed franchisees may have implications for the franchisor's support system, business model, or selection process. If that last one is systemic, it points to problems with quality control (too many dummies spoil the broth!) and future failures within the franchise system—maybe even your own. So be careful if every franchisee you speak with sounds as if they took one too many punches to the head.

When you do talk to these franchisees, ask specific questions. Ask them about their revenues—not just today, but when they started up. Ask them how long it took them to break even. Ask them about every cost element on the income statement. And, of course, ask them specific questions about the support provided by the franchisor. In particular, how helpful was the franchisor in the early stages of their business?

Stay away from generalities. Ask an easy question, get a meaningless answer. Try to avoid yes-or-no questions.

I have provided sample questions for your use in surveying franchisees in Figure 7–1 on page 150. These questions are intentionally arranged to start with broad, seemingly harmless generalities before moving to more specific questions at the end. This allows you to build trust with the franchisees before you start asking for details. And even if you do not get these latter questions answered, hopefully you will still have gotten some valuable information.

Remember, franchisees in general want you to join the system. When you enter the system, they gain advertising power and purchasing

Figure 7–1. **Questions for Franchisees**

These questions are only a starting point for your conversations with franchisees. You will need to supplement them with additional questions based on the specific franchise you are interested in. I recommend starting off with the easier questions to build rapport with the franchisee. You can ask the more sensitive questions once they begin to feel comfortable with you. Keep in mind that franchisees are busy people. While some may be willing to spend an hour on the phone with you, others may only give you 10 to 15 minutes.

1. How long have you been a franchisee in this system? What was your background before you joined as a franchisee? _____

_____

_____

2. What factors led you to decide to become a franchisee of the brand? _____

_____

_____

3. Can you tell me about the support the franchisor provided prior to your opening? Site location, design assistance, construction assistance, and training? What did they do well, and where did they fall short? _____

_____

_____

Figure 7–1. **Questions for Franchisees**, continued

4. How instrumental was the franchisor in terms of helping you build revenues in your first 6 to 12 months? What support did they provide that assisted in this? What else do you wish they would have provided? _____

_____

_____

5. On a scale of 1 to 10, with 10 being "excellent" and 1 being "poor," how strong do you feel the relationship is between the franchisor team and franchisees in this system? Why? _____

_____

_____

6. What are the franchisor's greatest strengths? _____

_____

_____

7. Where do you feel the franchisor needs to improve? _____

_____

_____

8. How does the franchisor share KPIs and operational best practices throughout the system? Do you feel the data helps you run a better business? Why or why not?

_____

_____

9. How frequent is communication among franchisees? How is it accomplished? Does it help your business? _____

_____

_____

Figure 7–1. **Questions for Franchisees**, continued

10. Do you feel the franchisor's consumer marketing efforts are productive? Why or why not? _____

_____

_____

11. How often are you visited by a field business consultant? Does that person have the skills and experience needed to help you grow your business and control costs? In what ways do they accomplish that? _____

_____

_____

12. How long did it take for you to become cash-flow positive in your business? Looking back, would you say the franchise was a good business investment for you? (If no, ask them why not.) _____

_____

_____

13. How many years did it take you to fully recover the investment you made in opening your franchise? _____

_____

_____

14. Do you feel the franchisor is genuinely concerned for your success as a franchisor? Why or why not? _____

_____

_____

Figure 7–1. **Questions for Franchisees**, continued

15. How responsive is the franchisor? If you call or email someone at the franchisor's office, do they respond to you quickly? Do they follow up on questions you ask them? _____

_____

_____

16. Would you mind sharing some general questions with me from your P&L?

_____

_____

17. What are your average monthly sales? Is there much seasonal fluctuation?

_____

_____

18. What is your cost of goods? _____

_____

_____

19. What are your labor costs? Do those include a full-time manager in the business other than yourself as an owner? _____

_____

_____

20. What type of location are you in (e.g., strip center, mall, kiosk, etc.)? What do you pay in monthly rent? How many square feet is your location? _____

_____

_____

Figure 7-1. **Questions for Franchisees**, continued

21. Would you mind sharing a copy of a typical income statement with me? _____

_____

_____

22. Looking back on the franchise opportunity, would you have bought this franchise if you could make the decision again? Why or why not? _____

_____

_____

23. What are the two most important pieces of advice you can give me as someone who is considering this franchise opportunity? _____

_____

_____

strength, as well as broader exposure of their brand name. But not all franchisees will be motivated to get you to join. For example, if you are speaking to a franchisee who wants to expand into the territory you're interested in, they may not want to be helpful at all.

Moreover, franchisees want to reinforce the decision they themselves made. Once people decide to do something, they want to find reasons to support that decision. In psychology, it's called rationalization. If we spend tens or perhaps hundreds of thousands of dollars, we don't want to feel like we made a mistake. We may overlook minor flaws in our purchase and rationalize them with overstatements of its good qualities. So too with franchisees. Be careful of their responses. In general, however, you'll find most franchisees are willing to share their honest experiences with you. And as you speak with more and more franchisees, you'll begin to see commonalities in their responses, which is another reason to speak with as many franchisees (and former franchisees) as possible. Their combined input will be the most valuable source of data in your due diligence process.

I have provided some questions you may want to ask franchisees in Figure 7–1, starting on page 150, but be sure to supplement them with questions based on information in the FDD, what you have learned through your own research, and anything else that might be relevant to the franchise opportunity you are considering.

What about new franchisors who have not yet sold a franchise? If you are considering becoming a franchisor's first franchisee, you need to satisfy yourself that the concept or the people behind it are ready for prime time—preferably both. And you need to exercise particular diligence when trying to estimate potential returns (covered in the next chapter). If there are no franchisees you can call, you need to factor that into your risk calculation—and be certain the returns offered more than make up for that degree of risk. That's not to say that being among the first franchisees in a system is a bad thing. Many franchisees have benefited from joining an emerging franchise system early in its development. It just requires an additional level of due diligence and a willingness to assume a higher level of risk in exchange for a greater anticipated return.

Using the Franchisor's Income Statement

A second method of estimating revenues involves the use of the franchisor's income statement, found in the FDD. While the franchisor will not disclose unit revenues in these statements, there are ways to make a guesstimate.

If the franchisor runs company-owned operations through the franchise company, there may be a revenue line in the statement reflecting revenue from corporate operations. If you can find it, simply divide that number by the number of units owned by the company to get average revenues per unit. This number will, of course, be influenced by any units that opened or closed during the period, but it will at least give you a rough estimate. Unfortunately for this method, most franchisors create a separate entity (or more than one) for corporate locations. This data is often not shown in the franchisor's income statement.

If there are no company operations, some income statements have a separate line item detailing franchise royalties. Dividing that number by the number of franchisees will yield the average royalty paid per franchisee. Divide the average royalty by the royalty rate, and you have an estimate of average revenue per franchisee. (For example, if the average royalties paid per store were $40,000 and the franchisor charged a 4 percent royalty, you would divide $40,000 by 0.04 to find an estimated average unit volume of $1 million.)

There are a couple of dangers in these methods. Watch out for the following:

- ✂ If company-owned units or franchises opened during the course of the year, both of these methods could understate anticipated revenues (since some units achieved less than a full year's performance). If you can determine how many opened during the year, you can cut that number in half and add it to the number of units open for a full year to give you a rough estimate. *Note*: Generally speaking, the more "young" units a system contains, the more revenues will be understated, as these units will typically be at the early stages of their revenue growth curve.

- ✂ Conversely, if franchisees ceased operation during the course of the year, chances are the number of franchisees would be accurately reflected in the disclosure document while the revenues might be inflated thanks to some income from these now-defunct franchisees. In this case, your estimate of your revenues could be overstated, since it would assume each existing franchise brought in more money than it actually did.

- ✂ Read the notes to the financial statements extremely carefully. Some accountants may lump franchise fees, royalties, and other fees together under "franchise fees." This will invalidate your analysis. *Caution*: Using numbers derived this way will overstate your anticipated revenues! Use these numbers **only** if you can back out all nonroyalty revenue.

✄ Another thing you have to watch for, especially with franchisors who have been around for a while, is changes in the royalty structure. If the franchisor has increased its royalties, some older franchisees may still be paying the lower rate. Using the current royalty for all franchisees would understate your anticipated revenues.

✄ If franchisees are not paying royalties (you can usually determine this by looking through the litigation section, if it has gone that far), revenues might be understated. Of course, you may have a larger problem to worry about.

✄ Finally, be careful you are not dealing with one of the franchisors whose royalties are based on gross margins. If you are, as is sometimes found in the temporary help industry, you can use the same formula to determine gross margin. But if the franchisor charges a flat fee, you won't be able to get any useful information, and if it derives its revenue from product sales, this method will not work. (You also need to watch out for franchisors charging a royalty or a flat fee, whichever is higher. When flat fees are paid in lieu of percentage royalties, estimated revenues will be overstated.)

Comparing Item 19 Data from Competitive Franchise Systems

If the franchise concept you're considering has an Item 19 disclosure, you can obtain FDDs for their primary competitors and see if they disclose the same type of information. For example, most restaurant franchisors typically disclose revenues, cost of goods, and labor. If you're considering a concept where the cost of goods is 32 percent and their direct competitors are all at 26 percent or less, that should raise a red flag. You should at least ask the franchisor why their cost of goods is so much higher than everyone else in the category. While there may be reasonable explanations for these variations (e.g., a franchisor may have a higher cost of goods because it uses better ingredients or intentionally charges lower prices), evaluating competitive FDDs will give you another point of comparison.

Using Performance Requirements

There may be other information in the FDD that can give you clues as to what the franchisor expects you to earn, often in the form of minimum performance requirements. If these exist, they would be disclosed in Items 6 and 12 of the FDD.

For example, the franchisor might have a performance requirement calling for a certain level of sales. Usually, franchisors with such a requirement use a relatively low estimate in the hopes that most franchisees would be able to meet it.

Many consumer service franchises (e.g., carpet cleaning, home inspections, etc.) require their franchisees to achieve minimum performance criteria to retain their franchise rights. If such requirements exist, they must be detailed in Item 12. For example, the franchisee may be required to achieve minimum revenues of $150,000 in their first year, $200,000 in their second year, and so on. Franchisors incorporate these requirements to assure themselves that an underperforming franchisee will not tie up a territory that should be generating much higher revenues (and royalties). If the franchise you're investigating has such requirements, you may want to compare them to the competition. You can also ask the franchisor how many franchisees have failed to meet the minimum requirements, and how it has responded to that. Have they terminated franchisees on this issue alone? Have they allowed underperforming franchisees to remain in the system but reduced the size of the protected territory?

Some franchisors, instead of using a sales-based performance requirement, may require a minimum royalty, as opposed to a percentage royalty—for example, the contract might specify a monthly royalty of 6 percent or $2,000, whichever is greater. While this is not a performance requirement per se, it does provide guidance as to minimum revenue expectations.

When a franchisor sets a minimum royalty requirement, it is generally an attempt to minimize the royalty erosion that could take place if a franchisee were to underreport revenues or to offset the franchisor's costs during the startup phase of a franchise. The franchisor's reasoning usually goes something like this: *Well, at a bare-bones minimum, every franchisee should be able to generate a minimum of $400,000 a year. At a 6 percent royalty, that would be $24,000 per year. So I'll charge a $2,000-a-month minimum royalty.*

Thus, if you want to derive that minimum sales number the franchisor had in mind when it set the minimum royalty, first annualize the minimum royalty payment by multiplying the monthly minimum by 12. Then divide the result by the royalty, as we did previously ($24,000 / 0.06 = $400,000), to get the franchisor's idea of a required minimum level of sales.

The danger in this method is that the franchisor may have grossly underestimated or overestimated the level of sales you should achieve, either because it is too aggressive, too conservative, or simply doesn't know any better. Thus, this methodology should be used more to confirm sales levels than to predict them.

Estimating Based on Observation

Another means of determining your estimated sales is through direct observation. While this may not work well for service-based franchises, where you can't stand in the location and observe lines of customers, you should be able to get a good feel for the sales volume of retail stores and restaurants if you have the patience.

This method is simple but time-consuming. Just go to a unit and watch people spend money. Even from outside the unit, you can count the customers going in and make an estimate, based on the average prices, as to how much each one will spend. Multiply average daily expenditure estimates by the number of days the establishment is open, and voilà! You have your estimate.

The downside to this method, aside from the time required, is the statistical aberrations that can occur when doing a limited sample. If, just by chance, you observe the unit on several especially good or bad days, your estimate could be off significantly. Thus, this method works best when you observe multiple units over an extended period of time.

Several cautions are in order if you choose this method:

- ✂ If the unit is location-sensitive or is affected by other variables you have not identified, your revenue estimate could be off. Try to observe units that are similar in most respects to the one you plan to open: similar locations, area demographics, size, etc. If it is a restaurant, the presence or absence of a drive-thru window could have a significant impact on revenues.
- ✂ If a franchisee is running a promotion or advertising heavily, it may impact your projections.
- ✂ Factors like the weather may impact your observations. Watching a business in inclement weather may result in an estimate that is too low, while watching only during good weather could result in estimates that will be somewhat high.
- ✂ Be careful about when you observe the unit. If you only go to a restaurant during the lunch hour, you may see a unit that is constantly busy, but only because you are observing during the rush. If you only watch it on the weekends, you may get a similar misimpression.
- ✂ Watch out for seasonality! Some businesses, particularly those in malls, may do more than 40 percent of their annual sales volume in November and December. Others may be heavily skewed toward summer usage or particular holidays.

While estimation by observation can provide you with a good deal of insight, it should be used to supplement and verify your other estimation techniques, as the small number of units you can observe (and the various aberrations that will almost certainly creep into your analysis) will limit the reliability of your data.

Estimating by the Book

Another (perhaps less accurate) alternative is to use industry averages to give you an approximation of these numbers. For example, some industry associations like the National Restaurant Association (https://www.restaurant.org/Home) or publications such as *Nation's Restaurant News* publish periodic guides to operating statistics that allow you to estimate an "average" unit's financial performance. Studies by the Risk Management Association, Dun & Bradstreet, and others can provide insight into a number of industries. (More information on these resources can be found at https://libguides.rutgers. edu/c.php?g=336557&p=2266142.) And of course, the internet contains reams of information—some of which may or may not be accurate—to help you with this research.

The danger in using industry averages to estimate your performance is that you may not achieve it—either because your franchise does not perform as well as the industry as a whole or because you underperformed. Likewise, in doing this research, often the categories into which your statistics fall (e.g., full-service restaurants, fast casual restaurants, etc.) may be too broad to be meaningful in deriving certain elements of your financial model. For example, McDonald's and Subway might both be lumped into the fast-food category, but their unit economics have very little in common.

Just Ask!

The last way to estimate revenue numbers is more direct—just ask. Even if the franchisor cannot answer your questions, others might. Try talking to the landlord for one of the system's franchisees. If you approach them about renting a space to house a marginally related business, they might give you an idea of how that franchisee is doing.

Most importantly, you need to ask other franchisees. They can be your best resources for questions such as these and are absolutely essential to your research process.

One last word of warning: Almost everyone you talk to has a hidden agenda, so everything they say should be treated with caution.

A franchise salesperson wants you to buy a franchise. A landlord wants to impress you with how high the volume in their property is. Even other franchisees have a hidden agenda: When you join the system, you increase their advertising and buying power. And most people don't want to admit it if they've made a bad decision. So be wary!

Nonrevenue Elements of Your Income Statement

As part of determining your income potential, you will also need to estimate the expenses (i.e., nonrevenue elements) you will incur in running your franchise business.

Again, the two best methods for deriving these expenses are to look at the franchisor's FPR (if it is listed) and speaking to existing franchisees (when they are available and willing to discuss these matters). But if these methods are not available to you, there are other ways to come up with a reasonable estimate.

Estimating Cost of Goods Sold

Your cost of goods sold (COGS) is, from an expense point of view, one of the most important figures you will need to determine. In a food-service business, for example, this would be the cost of the food and paper goods you use. In a retail business, it would be the cost of your inventory. In service businesses, you may have a negligible cost of goods sold. But determining your estimated COGS is not always as easy as looking at purchases in a given period—since what is sold in that same period rarely equates to those same purchases.

What you are looking for is the percentage of unit revenues that you anticipate you will have spent on whatever you sold during that period. Thus, if you establish your COGS will be 40 percent of sales, you can estimate that on $500,000 in sales, your COGS will be approximately $200,000.

If you want to determine COGS on a very granular level, perhaps in a retail business, you could start by looking at the selling price of a "market basket" of products sold by franchisees (and perhaps competitors). Then find wholesale prices online for those same products. Similarly, you can speak to wholesalers of various products to get their pricing (and perhaps their estimates of the COGS that others operate under).

One question you should ask is what your local competitors are charging. And, of course, you will want to see what other franchisees and the franchisor is charging for various services. This should give you a good idea of what you will be able to charge. Hopefully you have already taken this step.

This method, of course, does not work in certain businesses (like food service), where the franchisee combines products to resell them as a unique recipe made up of many different ingredients.

As discussed above, you can also use industry averages to give you an approximation of these numbers. The same publications referred to previously can be invaluable resources. But again, there are dangers in using someone else's numbers. Keep the following in mind:

✄ How were the numbers derived? If they were based on the pricing of a dominant industry leader and you're interested in a smaller franchisor, your franchisor may not have enough clout with its suppliers to get the same level of pricing.

✄ Were these numbers derived from companies selling different products than you will be selling? Or were they derived primarily from companies in substantially different markets? Both of these factors could throw off your calculations considerably.

✄ Has your franchisor taken such a large cut of your pricing by adding on a handling charge, retaining rebates for itself, or marking up the product (all of which should be disclosed) that your costs may be greater than industry averages?

✄ Or, alternatively, is the price negotiated by your franchisor better than you could otherwise achieve?

Finally, probably the best means of obtaining these numbers is again the most direct. In this case, though, after asking the franchisor, we will talk to some of its suppliers.

Estimating Labor

Deriving an estimate of labor costs is a fairly simple process, but it can very easily go wrong if you rely too heavily on shortcuts. Again, if the franchisor supplies an FPR, that is a good place to start in your hunt for a labor number. You can also, again, talk to franchisees about their labor costs.

However, those numbers may not be representative of what you can expect to achieve. Here are some of the things you need to consider:

- ✂ If you are looking at the franchisor's numbers, bear in mind that it may pay its employees based on its corporate wage scale—especially if it is a larger company. That might be significantly more than you would need to pay.
- ✂ Corporate labor, at least in some companies, may also be inflated by the lack of policies surrounding labor force reductions on slow days. For example, as a franchisee you would likely send employees home if the day was slow due to inclement weather. If the franchisor is not as aggressive, their labor numbers would be higher.
- ✂ If you are looking at franchisee numbers, they may choose to pay themselves a minimal salary and take money out of the business's profits. This is usually accounted for by showing just nonmanagerial labor costs, which at least provides some perspective.
- ✂ Likewise, franchisees may employ relatives in nonmanagerial positions at either inflated or deflated wage rates.
- ✂ Labor costs can be influenced by local economies as well. The Fight for $15, for example, has spurred legislation in New York, Los Angeles, Seattle, and San Francisco that will impact the minimum wage paid by you (if you live in one of those locations) or by the franchisor (or its franchisees) if it has a large number of workers in a $15/hour jurisdiction.

The other thing to be aware of is the relationship of labor in some businesses to revenue. In many service-based businesses, production labor can largely be treated as a variable cost. For every carpet you clean, you have an incremental labor cost. Fewer carpets, lower labor.

But in businesses like restaurants or retail operations, your labor often acts like a fixed cost, within certain ranges. While production operations like food service may see an increase in labor at higher revenue levels, there is a certain minimal level of labor required whether you get one customer an hour or 50. So if the location has lower sales, it might have very high labor costs. But a similar-sized location with very high sales may have very low labor costs. In talking to your targeted franchisor and its franchisees, you need to be sure you understand exactly how their labor model works.

Once you do, you can then focus on a more granular approach to calculating labor costs—using observation or input from the franchisor. When estimating based on observation, you need to be concerned more with the *number of hours* that are being worked than the costs involved. Watch units that are similar to yours in operation. How many people do they employ during peak periods? What about slack periods? (*Remember to be careful about factors such as seasonality.*)

Then start asking some questions. Ask franchisees how many man-hours are worked in their units or how many people are typically employed. Be sure they include all hours—including any that family worked without a paycheck. Ask them how their employees are compensated (hourly, salary, commissions, bonuses, etc.) as well.

Ask similar questions of your franchisor. It should be able to disclose this information without stepping over the line into an FPR. The franchisor can provide you with as much data as it wants on cost, even apart from Item 19, as long as it does not present it in a way that allows the franchisee candidate to use it to estimate profitability. So while a franchisor cannot provide you with costs as a percentage of revenues, they can provide you with estimates of monthly operating expenses without providing an Item 19 disclosure.

Then estimate the local prevailing wage for the individuals you will hire. Sites like Salary.com (https://www.salary.com/) can provide you with fairly decent estimates if the job title is commonly used. You may also want to check with some local noncompeting operations that hire employees of similar skill levels. Of course, if your state has minimum-wage requirements above the federal standard, you would need to be in compliance with those laws as well.

Again, the key is to estimate required salaries at various levels of performance. And if your salaries are not treated as a straight variable cost, figure out the minimum number of employees in a worst-case sales scenario, and then add employees to the operation in a stair-step approach to determine relative labor costs at various levels of sales performance.

Estimating Benefits and Taxes

Once you have your labor rate, you'll need to estimate the cost of additional payroll-related benefits and taxes. Some of these taxes will vary depending on which state you're in, but here are some examples for a business located in California so you can get an idea of what to expect elsewhere:

- ✄ Social Security (or FICA) is taxed at a rate of 6.2 percent of the employee's first $128,400 of salary.
- ✄ Medicare is set at 1.45 percent of the employee's total wage.
- ✄ Federal unemployment (FUTA) is set at 6 percent of the first $7,000 of an employee's wage.
- ✄ California's unemployment tax (SUTA) ranges between 1.5 percent and 8.2 percent of the first $7,000 of an employee's wage.
- ✄ Employment training tax is 0.1 percent of the first $47,000 of an employee's wage.

Of course, if you live in a different state (or even if you don't), you will need to check with your accountant to get the most up-to-date information on these expenses.

The biggest single benefit you can offer employees will be health care. In the current political climate, it is difficult to say whether employer-funded health care will continue to be mandated under the Affordable Care Act, and if so, at what level of employment. Depending on the number of people you employ and the current state of this legislation, you may want to consult an HR company, a payroll-processing firm, or your accountant to determine what might be mandated. In the case of health-care benefits, franchisees operate as any other independent business owner and decide on their own whether to offer them. If health insurance is not required for your employees, you will need to decide whether to provide it. Either way, if you plan to provide insurance, decide who will receive it and to what level you will fund it, and get quotes from insurance companies.

Another major benefit might include vacation. If you plan on taking one, or if you plan on granting a paid vacation to any of your employees, you must decide whether the business will need to hire people to fill in for those who are on vacation.

Altogether, the total cost of taxes and benefits, above an employer's direct wages, could be 25 percent to 30 percent in most states.

Estimating Rent

Generally speaking, this is one of the easiest categories to estimate. Many franchisors do not include rent when doing an FPR because it varies from market to market. But even if they do (or if franchisees are giving you detailed feedback), nothing beats a little legwork for accuracy.

First, ask the franchisor to provide you some information on the type of site you would need. How many square feet? What type of location (mall, strip center, street location, business center, etc.)?

With that information, you can contact some local real estate brokers and get a very specific feel for market rates. When talking to these brokers, you may want to question them on what kind of deals landlords would be willing to negotiate on what is called a tenant improvement allowance. Many landlords, especially in slow markets, will spend tens of thousands of dollars or more retrofitting or renovating your space (although this may mean you pay more for rent). If you're short on cash, this may be an option for you (although you will need to re-evaluate the business's return in light of these higher rents).

When it comes time to actually negotiate your lease, talk to neighboring tenants to find out what they are paying to get the best possible terms—but for now, you only need an estimate.

When speaking to real estate brokers, you may want to consider asking some of the questions in Figure 7–2. This worksheet gives you only a rudimentary look at the process of scouting locations, so supplement these with your own questions based on your research and the nature of the franchise opportunity. There are many good books on the subject you should consult before finalizing your location. And of course, you need to coordinate these activities with your franchisor. Bear in mind, too, that these questions are not designed to analyze a specific property but are instead meant to give you a feel for anticipated costs before you make your franchise investment decision.

Figure 7–2. **Questions for Real Estate Professionals**

You might start the conversation like this: "I am looking for _____ square feet of commercial property in a _____ (type of location: e.g., strip center, mall, street location, etc.) with _____ (description of traffic)." This information should be supplied by your franchisor or other franchisees. Then ask these kinds of questions:

1. What will I be paying for a good location (per square foot)? What is the availability of this type of property? _____

   _____

   _____

2. Does that figure include all associated costs (a triple net lease), or are those extra? What's included? Taxes? Refuse removal? Required advertising?

   _____

   _____

3. What will I have to pay when I sign the lease? (You should try to negotiate a lease that starts when you actually open your doors for business, not when you start the build-out. Since most landlords require a "date certain," the best you may

Figure 7–2. **Questions for Real Estate Professionals**, continued

be able to do is negotiate a start date beginning when you open your doors for business or on X date, whichever comes first.) _____

_____

_____

4. What security deposits should I anticipate on the lease? What are the utility companies asking for as far as security deposits? _____

_____

_____

5. Will you require my lease to be personally guaranteed? _____

_____

_____

6. What do utilities typically run each month? Does each space have a separate meter for gas and electric? _____

_____

_____

7. Do most landlords in the area provide an allowance for leasehold improvements on this type of property? Generally speaking, what does this run? How would this allowance affect my rental costs? _____

_____

_____

8. Are there any local signage ordinances I should be aware of? How will they affect my costs? _____

_____

_____

Figure 7–2. **Questions for Real Estate Professionals**, continued

9. What are the demographics of the area? Do you have any demographic reports you can share with me? _____

_____

_____

Estimating Utilities

The landlord or real estate broker can probably give you a good estimate of the property's electric and heating costs, so be sure to ask when you get your rent estimate. You should estimate high, of course, if the franchise requires an inordinate amount of electricity (if, for example, your franchise will operate in a large facility that will have substantial air conditioning requirements).

You will also need to budget for telephone usage. When you visit franchise units, try to determine how many incoming lines they have. The phone company can probably give you a good estimate based on the type of business you are interested in.

When you speak with franchisees, you can also ask them how much they pay in utilities per month. If they are a consumer-services business, their largest utilities expense is likely to be cell phones. If they are a restaurant, HVAC and electricity costs are likely to be most important.

The "Plug" Numbers

Next, include an allocation for any royalties, advertising assessments, or other ongoing fees charged by the franchisor. These fees should all be listed in detail in Item 6 of the FDD. And since many of these fees are expressed as a percentage of revenue or are otherwise predictable, you can generally just plug these numbers into your spreadsheet to know your exact expenses at any given level of sales.

For advertising, however, you may want to consider estimating slightly above the required assessment, especially early on, while you're building your business. If, for example, your business takes a while to get to break-even, you may want to ask your franchisor if an increased level of advertising will shorten that time frame. Often it is more economical to spend more upfront in advertising (assuming the dollars can be used efficiently) than it would be to spend less and do a slow bleed. You may also want to ask the franchisees you survey what they really spend on advertising and whether spending more sooner would help you ramp up faster.

Other Operating Expenses

On a business-to-business basis, other operating expenses can vary widely. These miscellaneous expenses can add up, so take them into account when making your projections.

Just some of the operating expenses you should investigate are:

- ✀ *Insurance.* You will need general business liability insurance, possibly auto insurance, and health insurance. Coverages will be specified in your FDD. You may also want to consider key man insurance or life insurance. Contact your agent for quotes.
- ✀ *Maintenance expenses.* You will need to maintain your unit to keep it looking like new. Ask people with similar businesses what they spend. Include things like refuse removal in this category.
- ✀ *Laundry.* If you have uniforms or linen, you will need to get them cleaned. Call a local service for quotes.
- ✀ *Vehicle expenses.* Calculating the cost of leasing or purchasing a vehicle is fairly simple if you know what you will be buying, but don't forget fuel and maintenance. If your employees will be driving their own cars, the IRS has a mileage allowance that indicates an appropriate reimbursement rate for each business mile.
- ✀ *Travel and entertainment.* While many think of this as simply a write-off, there may be necessary expenses that should be

included here. For example, your franchisor probably hosts an annual convention you will want to (or may be required to) attend.

✂ *Accounting.* If you're going to use an accountant or book-keeper to generate your monthly income statements and pay taxes, you'll need to estimate this.

✂ *Technology fees.* Ask the franchisor if franchisees need to pay fees to technology vendors, such as a CRM or point-of-sale provider. These can often be in the range of several hundred dollars per month. If these fees are paid directly to the providers rather than the franchisor, they will not be disclosed in Item 6 of the FDD.

Finally, ask your franchisor and the franchisees you speak with about other expenses they typically incur. Different types of businesses may have significant expenses not mentioned above, so be sure you have accounted for everything.

Depreciation and Amortization

To make a sound decision about purchasing a franchise, you may want to take depreciation and amortization into account—even though these are not out-of-pocket expenses.

Simply stated, depreciation is an allocation of the value that a physical asset loses over time, and amortization is a similar allocation for a nonphysical asset (such as goodwill). While they do not affect your pretax cash flow, they do affect your post-tax cash flow because after you purchase an asset (such as equipment), you can write off a portion of that purchase over time. Thus, depreciation and amortization will decrease your tax liability and increase your after-tax returns.

For most businesses, these items will have a relatively small impact on your financial analysis. But there are certain businesses where they play a more significant role. In the rent-to-own sector, for example, your ability to take accelerated depreciation on your inventory may put you in a position where you are cash-flow positive but have a significantly lower taxable income. You may thus be able to invest in an additional franchise (or additional inventory) and further increase your depreciation in subsequent years. In some businesses, you can pay little to no tax while growing your business year over year. And while the taxes will eventually catch up to you, you will have been able to accelerate your growth at a rate that you could not have otherwise, based on your reduced tax exposure.

Outside of this specific type of business, however, you should probably not take depreciation and amortization into account when calculating your return on investment. First, if you are incurring more depreciation or amortization, you probably spent more upfront. For example, you may have purchased rather than leased equipment. While examining this issue is certainly worthwhile, it is more of a finance decision than a franchise decision.

Second, when looking at the tax question, there are a myriad of different alternatives. But in an ROI analysis, the purpose is to compare alternative uses of capital. Not only would you need to consider different capital structures as they apply to the potential franchise, but you would also need to compare them to your alternative tax minimization strategies (buy vs. lease, etc.).

Debt Service

Like depreciation and amortization, debt service—the expenses you incur to cover the repayment of principal and interest on any loans you have taken out—is not an issue when you are developing your ROI model. Again, this is because the amount of debt you decide to carry is a finance decision—not a franchise decision. Moreover, the amount you might borrow could range between 0 percent and 70 percent or more—leaving you with a nearly infinite number of possibilities to test. From an ROI perspective, you want to look at cash returns vs. the total investment (even though you will likely want to finance some portion of your investment). This approach allows you to compare different investments without bringing your financing decision into the equation.

For businesses that will carry a significant amount of leverage, you *can* substitute a return on equity (ROE) analysis for an ROI analysis. An ROE analysis uses a similar equation as an ROI analysis, but substitutes the amount of equity invested in place of the total investment in the denominator of the equation. You will also need to adjust the numerator to reflect net income (after interest payments) as opposed to net cash flow. But if you are going to compare apples to apples in an ROE scenario, you must hold the amount (not the percentage) of equity constant.

ONE OTHER IMPORTANT NOTE: While you will not be figuring debt service into your ROI calculations in the next chapter, you absolutely must factor it into your ultimate buying decision. Owners' inability to handle debt service has been responsible for innumerable business failures, and you don't want to be among them. When conducting your analysis, you will thus use ROI to judge the quality of the franchise. But before buying, calculate your debt service and be certain you can cover it with your cash flows or additional savings, given a variety of worst-case scenarios. Otherwise, you're asking for trouble.

No One Can Eat Just One

Since you have already established your goals and over what time frame, now assess the projected financial results for each franchise to see if they will allow you to reach those goals. In some cases, the answer may be no, and you can narrow your list further.

But even if a single franchise cannot do the trick, remember that in some systems, you can open multiple units over a period of time. In assessing this option, you will first need to determine if the franchisor would sell you an area development agreement—or if it has additional territories in your geographic area that might be available to you once you have established your first location.

Assuming this is an option, develop a cash-flow model to illustrate how quickly the first location will achieve profitability, how much free cash flow it will generate, and how much incremental investment capital would be needed to open the second location. You can then incorporate that location (and any subsequent ones) into your planning process and reexamine whether your new game plan is viable.

Talk to Those Paid to Say "No"

One of the principles every buyer must follow is to understand the motivations of every seller. When someone is selling a house, they are motivated to show that house in the best possible light. Does that mean everything they tell you is untrue? Of course not. But you should still do a home inspection.

Similarly, you have now reached the point at which you should bring in outside expertise (if you have not done so already). When buying a business, hire people you are paying to say, "No!" Just as a home inspector is motivated to point out every wart and flaw, you need experts to help you evaluate the franchise opportunity.

Who are these people? And what are their motivations?

Start with your banker. Bankers get paid for making loans. If they can't put their money to work, they don't make money. So they're motivated to make loans. But the most important factor that allows a banker to make money is the percentage of bad loans. Too many, and they will find themselves in the unemployment line in a hurry. Thus, a banker's real motivation is to make only good loans. That is why most bankers are so conservative.

A banker gets paid to identify anything that can go wrong and be sure that the bank (not you) can recover from those mistakes. Since they do not want a loan to go south on them, they can serve as a professional skeptic—almost like a consultant you don't have to pay. Now that you have only a handful of franchise opportunities on your short list, you should once again approach your banker and present him with your preliminary financial analysis.

He may be able to point out flaws in your business plan or financial model. Or he may be enthusiastic about your prospects of obtaining a loan. Listen closely to what he has to tell you. But again, remember that he gets paid to make loans. And as long as he gets repaid (even if he has to go after your collateral), he will not be risking much.

Next, talk to an accountant. On a basic level, accountants are motivated by their hourly fees. What keeps them looking out for your best interests? Two things. First, you can't bill a lot of hours without delivering something of value in return. If your accountant comes back, says, "Looks great!" and sends you a hefty bill, not only will you never use her again, but you may not even pay her. And you certainly wouldn't refer others to her.

She wants to show you she knows her business, impress you with her acumen, and stun you with her brilliance. The best way to do that is to find every little problem and false assumption possible—and then charge you a hefty sum.

The second reason your accountant is a useful ally is that she has something to fear. You pay her good money to look out for your best interests. If you invest in that franchise and it turns out the financial assumptions she developed or signed off on were flawed, she knows she is likely to get sued (or, at a minimum, be subjected to scathing reviews on the internet). And no professional wants that.

If you have not yet hired an accountant, now is the time to sit down with one and go over your financial calculations line by line. Make sure she understands every assumption and underlying premise behind your calculations.

Finally, you should hire an attorney with experience in franchising. Like accountants, they have similar motivations for playing devil's advocate. They are paid to be deal breakers. Unlike accountants and bankers, however, do not get them involved in the process too early. While a good attorney will know more than just the law, many do not have an adequate understanding of the financial side of business—and that is not what you pay them for. Have a banker and an accountant do the number crunching before the deal gets into the attorney's hands. If the deal doesn't make financial sense, the contract really doesn't matter!

We will talk more about this in the next chapter, but if the deal makes financial sense, you should never sign any contract without showing it to your attorney. It'll cost a little now, but it may be the best money you ever spent.

Let me reemphasize one significant point here. The professionals you hire must bring quality advice to the table. That means they should have good, relevant experience. Of course, they will almost invariably tell you they have it. Get specifics! What franchises have they worked with? What references can they provide? Don't be afraid to interview multiple attorneys, accountants, and bankers to see if you want to work with them. Remember, they are vying to win your business.

THE BOTTOM LINE: CHECK YOUR HOMEWORK

I have said this before, but it bears repeating. Don't buy a franchise until you've looked under every rock and investigated every possible problem. One call to one franchisee is not enough. A day spent on the internet is barely a start.

Before you buy, have you . . .

- ✄ spoken with at least 25 franchisees (or all the franchisees if it is a smaller system)?

- ✄ thoroughly reviewed the FDD?

- ✄ run a Dun & Bradstreet credit report on your franchisor?

- ✄ visited multiple operating units (and most of the ones in your geographic area)?

- ✄ reviewed any website mentioning your franchisor? (Don't stop after a page or two of Google results.)

- ✄ thoroughly analyzed your current and potential competition?

- ✄ satisfied yourself as to the financial results you can achieve?

- ✄ checked your findings with professionals?

- ✄ evaluated social media review sites to see what customers think about the brand?

✄ thoroughly evaluated your risks and returns?

Before you make your final decision, you should be able to look at the list above and feel confident that you have done everything you could possibly do to investigate your choice. And based on that analysis, you should be in a position to make a reasonable estimate as to what you can earn in each of the franchise opportunities you are considering. If you still do not feel comfortable with your estimates, ask professionals for more help.

Chapter 8

MAKING THE LEAP

A t this point, you should have completed the following steps and narrowed your list down to a small number of franchise choices.

1. Assessed yourself and your ability to succeed as a franchisee (Chapter 2)
2. Assessed the risk associated with the investments you are considering (Chapter 3)
3. Developed a good understanding of the businesses you are considering (Chapter 4)
4. Determined if you are a good fit with the franchisor's culture (Chapter 5)
5. Developed an estimate of how much money you can make in each of these businesses (Chapter 7)

Now it has come down to decision time, which means it is time to get serious about the big picture. Have you found a match made in franchisee heaven, or will you keep playing the field? To bring all your research together and make that decision, you need to figure out your ROI.

ROI Analysis as a Means of Measuring Like Returns

At this point, you should be armed with the tools you need to begin comparing the franchises you are still considering from an economic perspective. The key tool is to conduct a return on investment (ROI) analysis. As alluded to earlier, your anticipated ROI is a measure of how much profit you expect to generate vs. how much you invest in the business.

Let's start with a basic understanding of how to conduct this analysis. First, as a franchisee, you are entitled to specific returns on each of the assets you employ in a franchise:

✄ If you own the land on which you will build your franchise location, you are entitled to receive rent at the current market rate. The assumption is that if you did not buy the franchise, you could rent the land to others or sell it (and receive a return on the capital you redeployed).

✄ If you plan on working in the franchise, you are entitled to a salary at the market rate. If you are the manager of the location, you are entitled to the same salary you would pay someone to do that job in your place. However, if you were an investment banker in your old life, don't expect to receive an investment banker's salary in your new job. Look at this model as if it were an investment and treat it as if you were a passive owner. After all, you could always get a job somewhere else and earn that salary while you invest your capital elsewhere to make a separate return.

✄ Since you will have to invest your capital in the business, you are entitled to an ROI commensurate with the level of risk associated with that investment. The assumption is that if you chose instead to put your money in a savings account, a bond fund, or a stock portfolio, each of these investments provides an anticipated return of a certain amount based on the perceived risk of each.

Using this process, you will be able to better understand the financial value proposition of different franchises. For example, if you read two FDDs and found that the anticipated return in one was $150,000 per year and in the other was $90,000, your first reaction might be that you would choose the franchise with the greater return. But if you had to invest $450,000 to achieve the return of $150,000 and only had to invest $180,000 to achieve the return of $90,000, you might change your mind. After all, you could buy two franchises that could return $90,000 each (remember, we are already assuming a manager's salary in our return calculations), or a total profit of $180,000 on an investment of $360,000. In that case, you would make more investing less money by choosing the second franchise. That comparison (of a 33.3 percent ROI for the first opportunity to a 50 percent ROI for the second) allows you to better understand the financial value of disparate investment levels.

Factor in Adjusted Anticipated Return

The first step in this analysis is to understand your adjusted anticipated return. In Chapter 7, you went through the process of determining your anticipated return. Take one more look at those numbers. Check that your model had a market rent if you will be using your own real property, and make sure you have included a market-rate salary for your own efforts. That will give you your return number, which you will use as the numerator in the ROI equation.

In conducting this analysis, it is often best to develop an anticipated-case, a best-case, and a worst-case scenario—and use all three in your modeling. This will help you better judge the upside potential and downside risk associated with the investment. But as you initially compare franchises, I would focus on the anticipated case. And your returns should be based on a "mature" level of revenues.

Determine Your Denominator

The next step is to determine the denominator—your total investment. Again, having already gone through this analysis in your review of Item 7 of the FDD, you should have a good baseline of what you think you will need to invest. When estimating your initial costs, you should always err on the high side, on the assumption that things will not go exactly as planned.

As part of that estimate, factor your sweat equity into your equation. In many businesses, the revenues and profitability grow over time. Assuming your business fits that pattern, you may need to take a salary below market rate during your first year or so of operation. While some of this may be accounted for as part of the Additional Capital line in Item 7, you should add back any sweat equity (the difference between a market salary and your planned salary) to your investment total. The rationale is that, again, if you did not make this investment, you could have a job at a full salary.

In determining the investment denominator, as discussed previously, you should probably assume an all-cash investment. At a later stage, you may want to conduct a return on equity (ROE) analysis, especially if the different businesses allow you to use different levels of leverage—but to measure pure returns, stick with cash-on-cash to start.

Measure Return as It Relates to Investment

Your next step should be to measure the return relative to the investment. Thus, divide the projected return by the amount of the total investment (at the top end of your estimated range). For example, if you conservatively projected an annual pretax profit of $50,000 beginning in your second year of operations, and you anticipated you would invest a maximum of $120,000 on this franchise, your ROI would be $50,000 / $120,000 = 41.7 percent.

You then need to decide if your projected ROI is commensurate with the risk associated with this investment. To do this, you must quantify other risks and their associated returns to see where your franchise investment falls.

For example, the return on a 30-year treasury bond (which has wavered between 2 percent and 3 percent over the past several years) might stand as a proxy for a no-risk, long-term investment. This is what is called the risk-free rate of return—since the government theoretically cannot default on this debt. Of course, an investment in a franchise is certainly not risk-free. Generally, you will find the return for bond funds a couple of points above the risk-free rate. Coming in at about 7 percent annually (again, looking at long-term returns, not short-term market fluctuations), you will find companies traded on the stock market. Since all these vehicles are available to you without lifting a finger (and can be more easily diversified to reduce your risk), your ROI should be substantially above that level.

Over the years, we have found the minimum ROI that tends to attract franchisees is in the area of 15 percent annually, with 20 percent returns being a more appropriate minimum for multi-unit investors. And, of course, the higher the better.

These numbers will vary at different levels of perceived risk (and for every individual making this investment). Moreover, they will change as competitive investments change (i.e., as interest rates rise or fall). But that should give you an idea, at least, of a reasonable starting point for a franchise ROI.

Finally, these figures do not account for the terminal value of the business (what you could sell it for when you decide to retire). They are designed to give you a way to compare the relative returns of different franchises, and do not account for long-term returns (which bring other factors into play). For example, some businesses might be easier to sell than others, and some industries might command different multiples.

If you plan to sell the business in the intermediate term, you should probably do either a present value analysis or an internal rate of return analysis, either of which would account for this selling price. Because establishing the future value of your franchise is difficult, however, you should enlist your accountant's help in conducting this analysis.

But ultimately, your goal is to measure each of your targeted franchise opportunities based on your anticipated ROI, so you can assign an anticipated return (and perhaps a worst-case number) to each.

Measuring Risk

With that done, your next step is to assign your assessment of risk to each of your finalists. Unfortunately, this is where you must get very subjective. There is no universally acceptable method of assigning risk to a franchise. We have spoken about numerous factors that can provide you with guidance, but no single factor or formula can quantify that risk.

In the world of franchising, many consider McDonald's the risk equivalent of a treasury bill—although even McDonald's franchisees have failed on occasion. One of the principles of good investment is that you should apply the risk-reward paradigm to your franchise investment decision.

If the franchise decision is between McDonald's and Joe's Burgers (assuming both are available, and both require similar investments), there can be only one reason to make McDonald's your second choice: You must believe Joe's will offer a superior rate of return. Moreover, this return must adequately offset the additional risk. Who in their right mind would invest in Joe's if they only hoped to gain an additional $1,000 per year? Even an extra $10,000? But would you do it if you expected $50,000 more a year? $100,000? $1 million?

Risk, of course, is relative, too. Burger King might be a higher risk in your analysis than McDonald's, but is it significantly higher? Perhaps not. In this case, maybe a difference of $50,000 per year would swing you one way or the other.

But if McDonald's is the proxy for the risk-free rate in the franchise world, how do we compare it to a carpet-cleaning business like Chem-Dry, where the franchisee simply buys a van and some equipment?

Obviously, if you have gotten this far, you have already eliminated any investment you felt was too risky. You have disqualified any franchises with more litigation, shady histories, poor management, or less experience than you are comfortable with.

Yet even after narrowing your list, risks will remain with all your chosen franchisors. And any of these risks—with the concept, market, management, or capital—can derail your best-laid plans. You must look at each and determine just how risky you feel the venture is.

Perhaps you develop a scale from 1 to 10. Or perhaps you just line them up in order, from least to most risky. But in the end, if you are going to invest in a franchise with more anticipated risk, it must also have a higher anticipated ROI.

Once you have completed this process, your decision should be fairly obvious. The franchise you want to invest in will be the one on your short list that offers the best balance (for you) between risk and anticipated return. But even after you have selected your final candidate, there is more work to be done.

Understand Your Obligations

If you have been following the advice in this book, by now you have already received input from bankers and accountants, your significant other is onboard, and you have perhaps spoken to a franchise attorney about some of the opportunities you are considering in general terms. But if you have not yet retained an attorney who specializes in franchising, now is definitely the time.

While a general business attorney may deal with a wide range of issues that support the needs of small businesses, I strongly urge you to select an attorney who spends the majority of her time advising franchisees and/or franchisors.

When choosing a franchise attorney, ask her how many FDDs she has reviewed (if you have to explain what an FDD is, move on). Ask if she typically represents franchisees or franchisors. Check that her website at least has some prominent reference to the word "franchise." And if she is a member of the IFA, all the better—it shows she is serious about her franchise practice. Bottom line, be sure you understand the depth of her experience before you hire her.

You should know upfront that many franchisors treat their franchise agreement as largely non-negotiable. The degree to which franchisors will negotiate varies substantially; it depends on the franchisor and on your negotiating power. If you are looking to acquire a large, multi-unit territory, you will have much more leverage than if you are investing in a single location. And if you are one of the first franchisees, you may be able to negotiate more freely than if you were negotiating with a franchisor with hundreds of locations.

Franchisors who refuse to negotiate have some good reasons. First, it is difficult to keep track of one's obligations when dealing with numerous individually negotiated contracts. Who would want to operate under 100 different contracts with 100 different franchisees and try to track their compliance with each? Second, negotiated changes in the contract, if significant, could create ill will with other franchisees if they feel you got a better deal than they did. And, given the nature of franchise law, if a franchisor negotiates any material changes in your contract, it will need to disclose them to future franchise prospects.

It is virtually impossible to negotiate with a franchisor on the material terms of a contract. But there may be areas where you can negotiate other terms as a risk-minimization strategy. You should try to find out whether the franchisor has any flexibility in its negotiating posture. Either way, you will want your lawyer to review the documents you will be signing so you can have a good understanding of your rights and obligations. You or your attorney should ask the franchisor early on how open they are to negotiation. You don't want your attorney to spend his time and your money developing a long list of provisions to change in the agreement if the franchisor is not willing to negotiate.

Regardless, be sure you understand the documents before you sign. Some of the typical provisions you need to understand are listed below.

- ✂ *Fees.* While it almost goes without saying, be sure you understand every fee and any purchasing requirements the contract obligates you to. If the franchise fee or royalty rate seems high compared to competitors, ask the franchisor why. If it can demonstrate that the difference in fees is because it provides a higher level of support, that's fine. If they don't have an answer, it's a red flag.

- ✂ *Noncompete.* Most franchisors include an in-term and post-term, noncompetition covenant in their contracts. These can be written very broadly and can make it very difficult for you to move on once the relationship has ended. They can also prevent you from owning complementary businesses during the term of your franchise.

- ✂ *Rights of first refusal.* If you sell your business, the franchisor often has a right to buy it at the same price and terms that have been accepted by a bona fide buyer. While this may not be a problem, if your eventual goal is to sell your business to a relative or friend, you will want to be sure you have that flexibility.

- ✂ *Approval of sale.* In the event of a sale, franchisors often have the right to approve the potential buyer. The logic behind this is that the franchisor would not want you to sell the business to someone unqualified or sell the business to a competitor. *Note*: You may want to try to negotiate a provision in your contract that will provide a future approved buyer with the right to sign a new franchise agreement in the event that you sell them your franchise (assuming the franchisor is still franchising), as this will provide a future buyer with some assurance that they, too, can get a return on their investment based on the length of their initial term with the franchisor.

- ✂ *Territory.* Understand the degree to which the franchisor or other franchisees can compete with you for business in your territory (if one is granted), either with the franchise concept or with another concept. Often these provisions give the franchisor some flexibility in the event that it acquires a competing chain. Most franchisors also reserve the right to sell similar products through other distribution channels. For example, if you're an ice cream store franchisee, the contract likely gives the franchisor the right to sell ice cream through grocery stores and convenience stores in your territory.

✂ *Grounds for termination.* Most franchisors spell out the exact grounds that give them the right to terminate your contract. Some of these provide for an opportunity to "cure" the default. Others do not. Most should be of no concern to you (e.g., convicted of a felony, abandonment, health or safety violations, etc.). Be sure you understand and can live with these potential issues.

✂ *Post-termination obligations.* These are your obligations should you be terminated or go out of business post-term. Most franchise agreements impose requirements on franchisees if they are terminated or close their business. These may include returning proprietary items to the franchisor, de-identifying the location as a franchise business, etc. Some franchise agreements also contain provisions for liquidated damages to the franchisor.

✂ *Personal guarantees.* Most franchise agreements contain some form of personal guarantee. This is often negotiated away for larger entities or corporations purchasing a franchise, but it is usually not subject to negotiation with individual franchisees. You should feel comfortable with the extent of the personal guarantee. Some franchisors also require all shareholders in the franchisee's business to sign a personal guarantee. If that is the case, anyone who is investing in your business must be willing to sign the guarantee.

✂ *Dispute resolution.* Make sure you understand the mechanisms and implications of the dispute-resolution methods in the contract (e.g., mediation, arbitration, litigation) and when different mechanisms are put into effect. In some companies, the franchisor will choose arbitration for the franchise agreement and call for litigation on any sublease or rental agreements—with cross-default provisions to the other contracts. If you withhold lease payments (putting you in default on your lease), you could be evicted, despite the fact that your franchise agreement calls for arbitration of any disputes. Be sure you understand how these situations might work.

✄ *Other contract provisions.* While less common, some franchise agreements may have clauses like an option to purchase your location or may give the franchisor other rights. Be sure you thoroughly understand these.

Remember, these will be written differently in each contract, so getting a precise understanding of exactly what each clause means in your case is vitally important before you sign on the dotted line.

Try to Negotiate a Stop-Loss Provision

While this is not true of all franchisors, one of the things you might want to consider in your contract-negotiation process is some kind of stop-loss provision. Depending on the contract you are looking at, you may discover it has a "Hotel California" clause: "You can check out any time you like, but you can never leave."

These clauses, depending on how they are written, might obligate you to operate the franchise unit for the entire term of the agreement. If this clause does not have provisions under which you would be allowed to cease operations, you might be required to operate a money-losing business for years. Or you could be obligated to pay the franchisor "lost future royalties and ad fund contributions."

If your franchisor has a flat-fee royalty built into its franchise agreement (say, a monthly royalty of $2,000) or a flat fee vs. a minimum, you can easily see how a franchisor might calculate these future lost royalties. But don't be fooled into thinking a percentage-based royalty doesn't work this way. Even if you go out of business, 6 percent of zero can be a meaningful number.

Depending on how the contract is written, the franchisor could still pursue you for lost future royalties. The courts have required franchisors to try to mitigate their damages, but the underlying theory is that it will take the franchisor time, expense, and effort to find a replacement franchisee (which is, of course, true). So while you might have eight years left on your contract, the franchisor may be able to recover projected royalties only from a fraction of those years. Nonetheless, you could spend a good deal of time and money in litigation—only to end up having to pay some portion of these lost future royalties. And if you have provided a personal guarantee (as you probably have), this could be a devastating blow after having invested much of your life's savings in a franchise that did not work out.

The solution is a stop-loss provision. You might negotiate a clause that says if you lose money on a cash-flow basis for two years at any time after opening, you can terminate with a given period of notice and without penalty. Or you might negotiate a lost future royalties provision that would limit or specify the amount of those losses upfront.

Of course, if you have to exercise this clause in the first place, it may already be too late to protect yourself, if you have gone all in on the purchase of your franchise. You may be secure enough in your investment decision that you are comfortable walking the wire without a safety net. But the key here is to minimize your risk as much as possible. And wherever you can reduce your risk or clarify language that may be ambiguous, you should do so.

If your contract is written in such a way that lost future royalties could be an issue, and Item 20 lists franchisees who have been terminated or closed their businesses, I recommend you speak with them on this issue. When they left the system, did the franchisor pursue them for lost future royalties? Some franchisors have this provision in the franchise agreement but do not consistently enforce it. Knowing the direction they've taken in the past may be helpful.

THE BOTTOM LINE: GET A FIRE IN THE BELLY—THEN FIRE YOUR BOSS

The time has come. You have narrowed your list and narrowed it again. You have done your homework. Called the franchisees. You are comfortable with the team and with the risk. You have calculated your expected returns. And you have gotten answers to all the tough questions. At last, you have chosen the franchisor that appears to be the best match for you.

Maybe you cannot wait to get started. Or maybe you are having some second thoughts and are still on the fence. But you will not hear me say, "Go for it."

Investing in a franchise is an intensely personal decision. You are risking your life's savings, throwing your career path out the window, and gambling with your family's well-being.

There are no guarantees in life, and there are even fewer when buying a franchise. Hopefully, this book will help you reduce your risks and increase your chances of finding the franchise that is right for you. But if it has only served to give you pause, only you can decide if franchising is the right decision for you.

No matter how hard you look, you will never find the perfect opportunity. Every franchise, like each of us, has its own strengths, risks, and potential rewards.

You are almost certain to wake up at night wondering if you made the right decision. You will worry about your future. And often the road to success will be bumpy. Things will likely go wrong. That is when you need to have the fire in the belly to make your business succeed.

Keep in mind that if you have followed the guidelines in this book, you have done your homework, so you have done virtually everything you could to make sure it was the right decision. And remember, these days working for someone else is less secure than it used to be, so the risk you have taken is relative.

Once you make the decision, make it succeed, despite any warts you may find later. In the end, if times get tough, the difference between success and failure will often be up to you. If things don't go exactly as planned, you may need to work long hours and make some sacrifices to succeed. But I can tell you from personal experience, as I expect every business owner can, that there is no greater satisfaction in the world of business than living the American Dream.

Chapter 9

THE DIE IS CAST

So you did it. If you are like most people, it took more than just research to make the decision. It took self-confidence and courage. And it may have taken some convincing of the people in your life—since they will be taking this leap with you.

Now you are on the hook. Bank loans. Personal guarantees. No job. No benefits. No security. Most of your life's savings invested in a venture that has not yet generated a dime in revenue. And you are betting the farm on a company and a management team you have known for perhaps three months.

Of course self-doubt has slipped into the equation. Maybe you are starting to have sleepless nights or starting to worry about early stage ulcers.

But you will get past it. After all, you have done your homework and found a business you enjoy with a team you trust. You have enough capital. And you know others have successfully navigated this path before you.

The best salve for your fear is to get to work.

Before your business opens, you should develop relationships with several franchisees whom you view as potential mentors. Most successful franchisees are more than happy to share their experiences, so don't be shy about maintaining contact with them to help you assess the early stage performance of your business.

And don't wait for the franchisor to get you started in the morning. While many franchisors will be all over you with an agenda of things you should be doing and when (many will have pre-opening checklists broken out in a countdown of weekly and daily tasks), you should get the process rolling as quickly as possible and set out to meet or exceed those deadlines.

While time was your ally before, now it is your enemy. The longer it takes to open your doors for business, the faster you burn through your capital reserves. In this chapter, I want to walk you through some of the initial steps after the ink has dried on the franchise agreement. This is not an extensive "here's how to run your franchise" chapter (in fact, that's a whole other book!), but rather a brief look at what comes next. Consider it an epilogue to your "I want to buy a franchise" story. Let's get started.

Creating the Franchisee Entity

In some cases, the franchisee entity may not be formed prior to signing the franchise agreement and the franchisor will be willing to assign the franchise agreement to a dedicated entity once it is created. If you have not done so already, one of your first tasks will be to create a new business entity.

There are numerous reasons for you to take this approach (as opposed to having the franchise be a sole proprietorship that you own personally). Most important, a separate entity will shield your personal assets from claims brought against your franchise operation. In fact, your franchisor will likely require this so that the franchise business is not mixed with personal or other business interests you may have.

There are various forms of entities, including a limited liability company, an S corporation, or a C corporation. Because your choice of corporate entity will have tax and ownership implications, you should consult with your legal, accounting, and tax advisors as to the most appropriate form to use. And if you are bringing on additional partners, you may also want to check whether your franchisor requires all partners of the franchisee entity to sign a personal guarantee, the noncompete agreement, or any other documents.

Obtaining Insurance

Your franchisor will almost certainly provide you with detailed specifications as to the amounts and types of coverage you will need to carry for your business. As one of your first steps, you should review those requirements with your insurance advisor. In speaking with your agent, you should anticipate that the franchisor will require it be named as an additional insured on your policy.

Take this opportunity to raise any questions you have with your franchisor. Your agent may also recommend some coverages over and above those required by the franchisor that you may want to consider.

Your franchisor may recommend insurance agencies. You may also want to check with other franchisees in your market/region to see which insurance firms they use, as they have likely done some competitive shopping on their own. Getting a couple of competing quotes may save you on your rates, especially if the insurance company is familiar with your business and your industry.

Site Selection and Lease Negotiation

Assuming that a physical site is important to your business, one of your most important tasks is finding the best location for your business. While you should expect that your franchisor will give you guidance, the ultimate decision will be yours. Your franchise agreement most likely contains language stating that the franchisor does not warrant the success of any location it approves. So if physical location and lease terms are important to your long-term success, treat this decision with the same level of due diligence that you treated your choice of a franchise!

As a first step, discuss with your franchisor what its recommended or required process is for site selection. It may have real estate brokers that you can (or must) use. If the franchisor requires you to use a specific broker, you should ask how she is compensated. In most cases, the broker is paid a commission by the landlord. If the designated broker is acting as the outsourced leasing department for the franchisor, they may charge an additional fee that you may have to pay.

If you use your own broker, be sure they have relevant experience. If, for example, you are opening a fast casual restaurant, a broker experienced only with quick service restaurant brands may guide you in the wrong direction if she doesn't understand the unique differences between these two categories. Don't assume that general industry experience will translate directly to the franchise business model you've invested in.

Assuming your broker does not have prior experience with your franchisor, have them schedule a meeting with both you and the franchisor so they fully understand the business concept and the type of real estate they should be pursuing on your behalf. This will save you time and increase the likelihood that the broker sources appropriate sites. Before you get too deep into the site selection process, ask other franchisees for input on site evaluation. What lessons did they learn? What do they like or dislike about the site they ultimately chose?

Ask the franchisor how it uses market analytics to help guide the site selection process. Analytics may include population, income, age profile, ethnicity, housing density, traffic patterns, drive time, competitive locations, and a host of other factors relevant to the franchise brand. A good franchisor should be able to guide you to a qualified source of market data that will help support any site decision you make.

As you evaluate potential locations, you should have a good feel for what target occupancy costs (i.e., total occupancy as a percent of sales) should be for the business. You can obtain this information from the franchisor and other franchisees in the system. *Note:* Once you have signed the franchise agreement, the franchisor is free to share financial data with you, as the rules regarding FPRs apply only to presale disclosure.

Once you have identified some sites you believe will work, the franchisor will almost certainly have an approval process for them. Submit your site or sites as soon as you have made a preliminary decision, as you will want to keep the process moving forward. If the franchisor provides you with guidance, you should listen closely. But it should not make emphatic comments about the potential success of any site unless it can back them up with market analytics.

Once the franchisor approves your location, you must negotiate your lease. The franchisor cannot provide legal advice to you during the leasing process. It is extremely important to retain an experienced local attorney who specializes in commercial real estate transactions to advise you and help negotiate the detailed lease terms with the landlord. If there are other franchisees in your market, ask them for referrals.

The next step will likely be to submit a letter of intent (LOI) to the landlord. The LOI is a short document that summarizes the key terms of the lease you're proposing. It is likely to include provisions such as a description of the space, the types of products and services you are allowed to sell, any restrictions on the use of signage or trademarks, your monthly base rent, any additional occupancy charges that will exist (e.g., common area maintenance), tenant improvement allowances (the landlord's contribution to building out your location to your specifications), the term of the lease, lease renewal provisions, and rent escalation over time.

As always, emphasize reducing your exposure in a worst-case scenario when negotiating your lease. While your landlord will almost certainly require a personal guarantee, try to limit it to a specific period of time. And bear in mind that the higher the tenant improvement allowance, the longer you will need to guarantee the lease.

Before you sign the final lease, the franchisor will likely want to review it to ensure that it complies with any requirements it has to protect the brand. Most franchisors will also request a copy of the fully executed lease for its files.

Finalizing Your Financing

While you probably began the financing process before you signed the franchise agreement, it may not be finalized until you secure a location or the franchise agreement is in place.

While a comprehensive treatment of franchise financing is beyond the scope of this book, bear in mind that many franchisors have developed lender relationships that may be of value as you look for financing. Ask the franchisor to provide you with a list of existing franchisees who have worked with those lenders, and ask them about their experience.

For most franchise systems where franchisees are likely to obtain SBA loans, the franchisor will likely be a member of the Franchise Registry. The registry enables franchisors to establish an ongoing relationship with the SBA and streamlines the process for review of individual loan applications from franchisees. More than 1,000 franchisors currently participate in the program. Details regarding the Franchise Registry can be found at https://www.franchiseregistry.com/.

Facility Design

Again, assuming your franchise has a physical location, the next phase will involve the design of your business location. Many franchisors require their franchisees to use a designated architect or to select from several preapproved architects. The benefit of this approach is that there is greater consistency to the design process and construction drawings can be developed and approved more quickly than if

every franchisee retained their own local architect. Additionally, using a smaller number of approved architects allows the franchisor to
negotiate pricing on behalf of franchisees.

If the franchisor allows you to source your own architect
locally, you should interview several before making your selection.
Your architect should have experience in creating construction
documentation for your type of business. Once you choose an architect,
the franchisor will likely provide him with base construction drawings
he can modify to fit your space. The franchisor will likely review all
construction drawings for approval before they are finalized. Most
franchisors do not permit architects to make material changes to
the core design elements of the franchise. Their role is to conform
the franchisor's design to the leased space you have selected. If your
architect has not worked with franchise brands before, make sure
he knows this so he does not waste your money trying to inject his
creativity into the design process.

Facility Construction

Once the architectural documents have been finalized, the next step
will be to select your contractor. You should only consider vendors
who specialize in commercial construction and have experience
building the type of business you're developing.

Most franchisors do not require their franchisees to use a specific
contractor. However, your franchisor may be able to provide you
with a list of contractors in your area who have worked with other
franchisees in the past. Again, other local franchisees will be a great
source of information on contractors.

As we have discussed in other areas, you should obtain multiple
contractor bids before selecting the contractor you'll work with. In
most cases, three to four bids are ideal. Your franchisor may have a
sample bid form you can use, which may make it easier to compare
bids.

As you obtain bids, also make sure you understand the timing
of payments that will be due to the contractor. And, of course, call

their references (or speak to franchisees who have worked with them). Learn whether there were cost overruns (and if so, how much they were and why they were incurred). Also determine whether the contractor started and finished on time. If there were delays, were they caused by the contractor or were there legitimate reasons outside the contractor's control?

Keep in mind how long it will take your contractor to complete construction. When obtaining bids, get an estimate of when your contractor can start and complete the project. And in selecting your contractor, do not just pick the lowest bid. If, for example, a contractor will take an extra month to complete your build-out, that is one more month you are burning cash while you wait for them to finish.

As you begin construction, ask the franchisor what communication they will maintain with you and the contractor. A representative of the franchisor will typically visit one or more times during construction. The frequency of these visits will vary depending on the type of business you're building (e.g., a tax office vs. a casual dining restaurant). In almost all cases, the franchisor will undertake a thorough inspection of the location as construction is completed to approve the business for opening and will prepare a final list of items to complete (or change) for the contractor. This usually happens just before the franchisor's training team arrives to help the franchisee prepare for opening.

Setting Up a Home Office

If your business will be run from a home office, the franchisor will likely have guidelines or requirements for setting up your office. Regardless of those guidelines, make sure the office has a closed door and is away from pets and children. You need to establish a professional environment where you can focus on your business. Check with your franchisor as to any requirements for a fax, landline, IP phone system, computer, software, etc.

You will also want to speak with your accounting/tax advisors about how your home office will be treated from an expense and tax perspective. Some portion of your monthly home bills may be tax-deductible.

Accounting and Payroll Processes

Once your franchise entity is established, you will also want to decide how to set up your accounting and payroll processes. Your franchisor may recommend or require specific accounting software that you or your bookkeeper should use. Many franchisors have national account programs with payroll service companies such as ADP or Paychex and will negotiate rates and terms of service on behalf of their franchisees.

In high-performing systems, the franchisor almost always establishes specific accounting guidelines for franchisees. If franchisees use the same format for their chart of accounts and income statements, it makes it easier for the franchisor to collect, analyze, and benchmark income statements for the entire system. As a franchisee, it benefits you to be able to compare your monthly income statement against the performance of the entire franchise network. Financial transparency also helps the franchisor identify strengths and weaknesses in the system and better coach franchisees where their business may be operating below average.

If you do not have prior accounting or bookkeeping experience, it's a good idea to outsource that function to a professional. As a new business owner, your time will be much better spent hiring great employees and managing the business, rather than learning how to use accounting software and making journal entries.

Creating an Initial Operating Budget

As you prepare to open your business, you should create a budget for your first 6 to 12 months of operation. The budget should provide you with a road map of benchmark targets for key performance measures such as customer counts, average sales price, revenues, cost of goods, gross margins, and key operating expenses (such as rent, payroll, and marketing). After you sign the franchise agreement, your franchisor should be open to assisting you in the budgeting process. It would also be helpful to speak with other franchisees who have been operating for perhaps one to two years. Their experience will help you develop key assumptions for the budget.

One important factor to consider in developing the budget is your personal compensation. Some businesses drive revenue and profitability very early in their life cycle, while others take much longer. Your budget should factor in when you can begin to take a salary and how much you should take. While you can minimize certain taxes and fees that are based on your salary (such as Social Security, Medicare, and unemployment insurance) by minimizing your compensation and taking profit distributions instead, the IRS has requirements for "reasonable compensation." Check with your accountant to obtain guidance on an appropriate salary at various stages of your business's development.

Integration with Key Suppliers

In the weeks or months leading up to your business opening, you'll want to develop relationships with each of your key suppliers. Your franchisor will likely have a list of required and recommended suppliers. Some of these suppliers may require you to establish credit terms with them. As you get to know each supplier, you'll learn their processes for ordering, delivery, quality control, product returns, customer service, and payments.

The franchisor may have also negotiated with suppliers that will work with your contractor during the construction process. For example, your contractor may be required to purchase equipment, lighting, flooring, millwork, and other items from designated suppliers, which he will install during construction. Also, deliveries from other suppliers, such as kitchen equipment, may need to be arranged during construction. Some coordination between your suppliers and your contractor may be necessary.

Hiring and Training Your Team

If you will hire a staff before you begin operations, this is one of the most critical issues you should focus on. In most businesses, franchise or not, the quality of the team will drive success. Your franchisor should recommend which staff positions need to be filled before opening day. Existing franchisees can provide input on what to look for as you hire employees, the process you should use to recruit and evaluate potential hires, and strategies for your salary and bonus structure.

This is one area, however, where most franchisors will steer clear of any direct involvement to avoid the vicarious liability that joint employment or an agency relationship might create. For this same reason, your franchisor will typically have little to no involvement in training any of your staff below the management level. So while you may get guidelines, recommendations, and job descriptions, this responsibility will fall on you.

For this reason, your franchisor will often not provide you with an employee handbook (or if it does, it will only be a recommended format—you will still need to write the policies). You may want to hire an HR firm or an employment attorney to help you create this document early in the hiring process.

Depending on the type of business you're opening, it is often wise to overstaff at the beginning, with the expectation that not all the employees you hire will stay or perform at a satisfactory level during the initial weeks or months of operation. Additionally, since your team will have limited experience the day you open your doors, overstaffing will allow you to provide a faster (and presumably better) consumer experience. If you go this route, be sure you account for it in your budgeting process.

In speaking with franchisees over the past several decades, it was rare to hear from an owner who felt paying above-market wages was a mistake. High levels of turnover can result in higher recruitment costs, higher training costs, and, most insidiously, poor customer service—which ultimately translates to lost customers. Good business leaders hire capable people, pay them well, and provide effective leadership to their team. Franchisees who fail to recognize the cost of turnover often struggle. As you determine your wage scale, be sure to consider these soft costs.

Planning Initial Marketing Activities

Your franchise agreement will likely require you to spend a minimum amount of money on marketing over the first 30 to 90 days of operation. Your franchisor will likely advise you on which strategies will be most useful for building your business in those first critical months. They will often have one or more third-party vendors who can assist in planning and executing your initial marketing. Many franchisors today outsource digital marketing, social media, and public relations, as it is often beneficial to centralize functions where a single knowledge base can be established to advise franchisees, develop content, and negotiate media rates.

Like hiring the best people and overstaffing, this is another area where you are often well-advised to exceed the minimal standards. Assuming your marketing is effective, the more marketing dollars you spend initially, the faster you will grow your business and achieve profitability. Remember, again, that time is your enemy until you start making a profit. If you overspend early and get to break-even and beyond faster, you may actually save money by reducing your operating losses over time.

In determining your budget and your marketing plan, you should again speak with existing franchisees who have been in operation one to two years. In addition to the franchisor's feedback, they should be able to provide you with useful benchmarks and appropriate expectations based on the media you employ. Understanding what has and has not worked for other franchisees will help you maximize your success and minimize waste in your initial marketing spend.

Training at the Franchisor's Location

In addition to advising you how many staff positions should be filled, the franchisor will require certain employees from your organization to attend operations and business training before opening day. This training is typically provided at or near the franchisor's home office, either in a dedicated training facility or in a business location owned and operated by the franchisor or its affiliate. In some cases, the franchisor will allow additional staff to attend, so depending on how many people you've hired prior to the training, you may want to bring more employees with you. While this means an added expense, there is a tremendous benefit to exposing more of your staff to the franchisor's training program.

A few franchisors delegate training to other franchisees. This is not considered best practice, however, as franchisees tend to inject their personal biases into the training process.

As you and your team attend training, you'll want to take full advantage of the knowledge and resources available to you. At the conclusion of training each day, consider getting together with your team to discuss what you learned and develop a list of follow-up questions for the franchisor.

Training at Your Location

The second phase of training for many franchisors occurs around the opening of the franchise business. The length and content of training at your location will, of course, depend on the training needs specific to your business. If you are going to be operating a service business such as lawn care, home improvement, or commercial services, the focus of training within your territory will likely be on sales and customer service. The trainer will often spend several days with you conducting grass-roots marketing, following up on sales leads, undertaking sales presentations, and performing services at the customer's location. If you are operating a retail business or restaurant, training will focus on preparing the facility to open and four-walls operations training for your staff.

The objective of a franchisor training program is to equip you to implement the franchisor's processes in your business over time. Since the franchisor's trainer (or training team) will only be at your business for a limited amount of time, the focus of training during the first several days is typically on operational execution and ensuring that your first customers receive proper service. Toward the end of the on-site training process, the focus shifts to observing your and your key staff's ability to manage other employees in their day-to-day tasks.

Priorities in the Early Months

For most new franchisees, the first 6 to 12 months of operations should focus on building revenues, developing a solid staff, and executing well against the franchise brand relative to quality and the overall customer experience. While cost controls should be maintained, they should not be the primary focus.

It is critical to generate monthly income statements and share that information, along with any other performance metrics (e.g., point-of-sale data), with the franchisor. The franchisor's field business consultant should work with you as you build your business to review your progress on the budget you prepared. The franchisor and its team have more experience than you do on how your business should perform over the first 6 to 12 months. I highly recommend that you maintain close contact with the franchisor's team to measure and assess your performance.

THE BOTTOM LINE: MAKE YOURSELF OBSOLETE AND YOUR MANAGERS REDUNDANT

Finally, one more piece of advice. Unless you are looking to "buy yourself a job," your most important goal should be to make yourself unnecessary. That means you need to hire and train people to run the operation even though you could do it yourself and pocket their salary instead. It also means developing a program to train up additional managers in that same role, so if you lose the first manager who has taken over for you, there is always another one waiting in the wings to take over.

Make no mistake, this strategy will cost you in the short term. But one step backward now will allow you to take two steps forward in the future.

Making yourself unnecessary to the operation will allow you to focus on building your business instead of focusing on your job. If you get run over by a bus, have a serious health issue, or just want some time for your family, your business will still provide you with an income despite your absence. But if you instead decide to grow your business, this strategy will give you the cash flow to finance your growth and give you the time you need to open a second franchise.

Most people will tell you that when it comes to expansion, the second unit is the most difficult. You will have the least amount of cash flow and the fewest qualified managers to leverage, and it will be your first experience with multi-unit ownership. But once you get past number two, you are in a better position to develop more and more, putting you on the road to true long-term financial independence.

To borrow from the popular maxim, when you can work on your business instead of in it, you will be well on your way to franchise prosperity.

RESOURCES

Franchise Directories

Business Opportunities Handbook (https://www.busopl.com/)

Franchise Times Book of Brands (http://www.franchisetimes.com/Store/Book-of-Brands/)

IFA Popular Franchise Opportunities (https://www.franchise.org/franchise-opportunities)

The Franchise Handbook (https://www.franchisehandbook.com/)

Franchise Portals

America's Best Franchises.com (https://americasbestfranchises.com/)

AZFranchises.com (http://www.azfranchises.com/)

BeTheBoss.com (https://www.betheboss.com/)

BizBuySell.com (https://www.bizbuysell.com/)

BizQuest (https://www.bizquest.com/)

Business Broker Network (https://www.businessbroker.net/)

Business Opportunities Handbook: Online (https://www.busopl.com/)

BusinessesForSale.com (https://www.businessesforsale.com/)

BusinessMart.com (https://www.businessmart.com/)

Entrepreneur (https://www.entrepreneur.com/)

FastCasual.com (https://www.fastcasual.com/)

FindaFranchise.com (https://www.findafranchise.com/)

FoodFranchise.com (http://foodfranchise.com/)

FoodTruckOperator.com (https://www.foodtruckoperator.com/)

Franchise Action Network (https://www.franchise.org/)

Franchise Buy (https://www.franchisebuy.com/)

Franchise Buyers Network (https://www.franchisebuyersnetwork.com/)

Franchise Direct (https://www.franchisedirect.com/)

Franchise Gator (https://www.franchisegator.com/)

Franchise Genius (https://www.franchisegenius.com/)

Franchise Post (http://franchisepost.com/)

Franchise Solutions (https://www.franchisesolutions.com/)

Franchise Times (http://www.franchisetimes.com/)

Franchise.com (https://www.franchise.com/)

FranchiseClique.com (https://www.franchiseclique.com/)

FranchiseForSale.com (https://www.franchiseforsale.com/)

FranchiseHarbor (http://www.franchiseharbor.com/)

FranchiseHelp.com (https://www.franchisehelp.com/)

FranchiseOpportunities.com* (https://www.franchiseopportunities. com/)

Franchiseroom.com (https://www.franchiseroom.com/)

FranchisesforSale.com (http://www.franchisesforsale.com/)

FranchiseWorks.com (http://www.franchiseworks.com/)

Franchising.com (https://www.franchising.com/)

Franchisingwomen.com (https://www.franchisingwomen.com/)

Key4money.com (https://www.key4money.com/)

PizzaMarketplace.com (https://www.pizzamarketplace.com/)

QSRweb.com (https://www.qsrweb.com/)

The Franchise Handbook (https://www.franchisehandbook.com/)

TheFranchiseMall.com (http://thefranchisemall.com/)

Trade Shows

Franchise Expo Midwest
Inaugural show in 2018, held in Chicago
https://www.franchiseexpomidwest.com/

Franchise Expo West
Typically held in Southern California
https://www.franchiseexpowest.com/

Franchise Expo South
Venues vary, held most recently in southern Florida
https://www.franchiseexposouth.com/

Franchise Times Finance & Growth Conference
Typically held in Las Vegas
http://www.franchisetimes.com/Conferences/The-Franchise-
Finance-Growth-Conference/

Franchise Update Multi-Unit Franchising Conference
Typically held in Las Vegas
https://www.multiunitfranchisingconference.com/

IFA Annual Convention
Venues vary, but held in Las Vegas every other year
https://www.franchise.org/convention

International Franchise Expo (IFE)
Typically held in New York City
https://www.ifeinfo.com/

The Franchise Expo/The Franchise Show
Multiple venues across the U.S. and Canada
http://www.franchiseshowinfo.com/ or http://www.nationalevent.
  com/

The Great American Franchise Expo
Multiple venues across the U.S.
https://www.franexpousa.com/

Associations and Helpful Organizations

International Franchise Association (IFA)
  https://www.franchise.org/

SCORE
  http://nationalbusiness.org/score-association/

U.S. Small Business Administration (SBA)
  https://www.sba.gov/

WHERE TO OBTAIN AN FDD

This book extensively discusses the franchise disclosure document (FDD) used in franchising. Below are the resources we use to obtain FDDs in our own franchising business.

California—FREE
https://docqnet.dbo.ca.gov/search/

Minnesota—FREE (Historical FDDs are available too.)
https://www.cards.commerce.state.mn.us/CARDS/

Wisconsin—FREE (This is the most user-friendly site, with clean FDDs available.) https://www.wdfi.org/apps/FranchiseSearch/MainSearch.aspx

FranchiseDisclosures.com
Provides FDDs for $150 apiece. Item 19s are available as well. http://www.franchisedisclosures.com/

FRANdata

Provides FDDs for $220 apiece.
https://shop.frandata.com/fdd/

The Educated Franchisee FDD Exchange

Membership-based, although you can review one FDD for free every 24 hours. More requires a monthly fee.
https://fddexchange.com/

SAMPLE CONFIDENTIAL INFORMATION REQUEST FORM (CIRF)

S ome franchisors may ask you to complete a confidential information request form (or CIRF, although some franchisors may
just call it an application) that will provide the franchisor with
more details on your qualifications. This form is generally completed
as a first step in the franchisor's qualifying process.

The form on the following pages is a sample that will illustrate
the kind of information that a franchisor will generally request.

Submit to:

XYZ Franchise Company
Address
Phone:
info@
www.

**Confidential
Information
Request
Form**

Last Name	First Name	Middle Name	Social Security Number

Date of Application (MM/DD/YY)	Birth Date (MM/DD/YY)	Age	Email address	Telephone Number ( )

Current Address	City	State	ZIP	How long?

Previous Address	City	State	ZIP	How long?

Marital Status	Full Name of Spouse	Occupation of Spouse

Names and Ages of Dependent Children

Name	Age
Name	Age
Name	Age
Name	Age

APPLICANT'S FRANCHISE PLANS

Will the franchise be owned and operated by you or a group?
Please explain fully
Amount of capital available for this business
Describe fully

Territory for which application made	Would you consider any other area?
What area(s)?	

THIS IS NOT A CONTRACT AND SUPPLYING OR COMPLETING THIS FORM INCURS NO OBLIGATION ON EITHER PARTY.

EDUCATION

Name of School	Dates of Attendance (MM/DD/YY) To	Major & Minor Fields	
Location of School	Grade Average or Class Standing	Diploma or Degree	Date of Graduation (MM/DD/YY)
Name of School	Dates of Attendance (MM/DD/YY) To	Major & Minor Fields	
Location of School	Grade Average or Class Standing	Diploma or Degree	Date of Graduation (MM/DD/YY)

BUSINESS & EXPERIENCE RECORD

Have you been in business for yourself?

Name & Address Of Employer

Position, Title & Duties

Dates Of Employment	From: (MM/DD/YY)	To: (MM/DD/YY)	

Supervisor's Name & Title

Reason for Separation		Beginning salary $	Ending salary $

Name & Address Of Employer

Position, Title & Duties

Dates Of Employment	From: (MM/DD/YY)	To: (MM/DD/YY)	

Supervisor's Name & Title

Reason for Separation		Beginning salary $	Ending salary $

Name & Address Of Employer

Position, Title & Duties

Dates Of Employment	From: (MM/DD/YY)	To: (MM/DD/YY)	

Supervisor's Name & Title

Reason for Separation		Beginning salary $	Ending salary $

PHYSICAL CONDITION

General Physical Condition	Date of Last Physical Exam

List Any Physical Impairments Or Chronic Illnesses Which May Preclude Certain Types Of Activities
Explain

"I submit the foregoing information as my complete and true personal and financial condition as of the date shown below. In accordance with the Privacy Act (5 U.S.C. 552 a), Freedom of Information Act and The Fair Credit Reporting Act, I expressly authorize any past or present employer, any law enforcement agency, federal, state or local, or any person who has personal knowledge of my character, work experience or criminal records to release this information to the Franchisor. If requested by the Franchisor, I agree to supply statements from my professional advisors (i.e., banker, broker, accountant or attorney) verifying the above assets, and I also agree to furnish copies of Federal Income Tax Returns as filed for the last five years. I understand that the Franchisor is relying upon all the above information as a material factor in considering my application to become a franchisee, and I therefore agree to promptly notify the Franchisor of any material change in any of the above information or any subsequent information provided to franchisor. In addition, I release all persons from liability as a result of true, accurate information. Further, Franchisor confidential information and trade secrets will not be disclosed by Applicants to any other person or business entity, and will not be used by Applicants in any manner outside the evaluation process, either during or after the evaluation process."

Signature   Date

REFERENCES

PLEASE LIST THREE PROFESSIONAL & CHARACTER REFERENCES.

1. Name		Address		Telephone	( )
2. Name		Address		Telephone	( )
3. Name		Address		Telephone	( )

PLEASE LIST THREE CREDIT REFERENCES.

1. Name		Address		Telephone	( )
2. Name		Address		Telephone	( )
3. Name		Address		Telephone	( )

BANK REFERENCES

1. Name		Address		Telephone	( )

CRIMINAL BACKGROUND

Have you ever been convicted of a felony?! ☐YES ☐NO	If yes, please explain

INCOME

YEAR	
EARNED (salary, commissions, fees, etc.)	$ __
INTEREST & DIVIDENDS RECEIVED	$ __
RENTS RECEIVED	$ __
OTHER INCOME	$ __
	$ __
—	$ __
	$ __
GROSS INCOME	$

CONTINGENCIES

Do You Have Any Contingent Liabilities? ☐YES ☐NO
If So, Please Itemize:

Are Any of Your Assets Pledged? ☐YES ☐NO
Describe:

Are You a Defendant in Any Suits or Legal Actions? ☐YES ☐NO
Describe:

CONFIDENTIAL FINANCIAL STATEMENT   DATE: YEAR: 20   PLEASE ANSWER ALL QUESTIONS USING "NO" OR "NONE"
WHERE NECESSARY

ASSETS		LIABILITIES AND NET WORTH	
Cash on Hand & Unrestricted in Banks (See Sched. No. 1)	$	Notes Payable to Banks, Unsecured Direct Borrowings Only (See Sched. No. 1)	$
U.S. Government Securities	$	Notes Payable to Banks, Secured Direct Borrowings Only (See Sched. No. 1)	$
Accounts & Loans Receivable (See Sched. No. 2)	$	Notes Receivable, Discounted with Banks, Finance Companies, etc.	$
Notes Receivable, Discounted With Banks, Finance Companies, etc. (See Sched. No. 2)	$	Notes Payable to Others, Unsecured	$
Life Insurance, Cash Surrender Value (Do not deduct loans) (See Sched. No. 3)	$	Notes Payable to Others, Secured	$
Other Stocks & Bonds (See Sched. No. 4)	$	Loans Against Life Insurance (See Sched. No. 3)	$
Real Estate (See Sched. No. 5)	$	Accounts Payable	$
Automobiles Registered in Own Name	$	Interest Payable	$
Other Assets (itemize)	$	Taxes & Assessments Payable (See Sched. No. 5)	$
		Mortgages Payable on Real Estate (See Sched. No. 5)	$
		Other Liabilities (itemize)	$
TOTAL ASSETS	$	**TOTAL LIABILITIES**	$
		NET WORTH	$

THIS IS NOT A CONTRACT AND SUPPLYING OR COMPLETING THIS FORM INCURS NO OBLIGATION ON EITHER PARTY.

GLOSSARY

ad fund—Established by the franchisor, an ad fund is a pooling of prescribed advertising fees within a franchise system in order to carry out marketing.

area development—An area development (also referred to as a multi-unit) franchise is similar to an option agreement, in which the area developer is granted an exclusive option to open a pre-established number of franchises in a defined geographical area, according to a specified schedule. Under an area development strategy, the franchisee must execute a separate franchise agreement for each location he opens within the protected area.

confidential information request form (CIRF)—A form filled out by franchise prospects providing details on their qualifications. See Appendix C for a sample.

Discovery Day—A one-on-one meeting at which a prospect is formally disclosed and a detailed discussion about the sale of the franchise takes place at the franchisor's place of business.

Federal Trade Commission (FTC)—The federal agency responsible for regulating franchising under the Franchise Rule.

financial performance representation (FPR)—A representation of sales or earnings that is sometimes made in Item 19 of the FDD, almost always based on historical financial performance of the franchisor or an affiliated entity.

franchise—Defined by the FTC, this includes any agreement where the franchisee obtains the rights to operate a business associated with the franchisor's trademark, the franchisor exerts control over or provides significant assistance to the franchisee's method of operation, and it requires the franchisee to pay a fee to the franchisor or an affiliate.

franchise broker—A person who: i) is under contract with the franchisor relating to the sale of franchises; ii) receives compensation from the franchisor related to the sale of franchises; and iii) arranges franchise sales by assisting prospective franchisees in the sales process. There are two different types of broker networks. Lead referral networks (often called franchise brokers) pre-qualify candidates and refer them to a franchisor's sales team, which then shepherds the prospect through to the final sale. Alternatively, franchise sales outsourcing firms also qualify under this broad definition.

franchise disclosure document (FDD)—A document much like a securities offering that has 23 specific points of disclosure, which must be provided to a prospective franchisee 14 calendar days before the execution of a franchise contract or the acceptance of funds from that prospective franchisee.

franchisee—A franchisee is a person or entity who buys a franchise.

franchisor—A franchisor is any person or entity who grants a franchise and enters into a franchise relationship with a franchisee.

protected territory—An area granted to a franchisee in a franchise agreement where the franchisee will have defined levels of exclusivity without encroachment from others operating in the system.

return on investment (ROI)—A formula to determine the percentage of the initial investment that is recaptured in a period of time (in this book, we look at annual ROI figures), to compare the relative performance of investments.

royalty—Regularly occurring payments made by a franchisee to a franchisor, often (but not always) based on a percentage of revenues.

single-unit franchise—A single-unit franchise is the most common form of franchising within the U.S. and involves awarding a single franchise to an individual or company that may or may not have prior experience in the franchisor's industry.

ACKNOWLEDGMENTS

Over the course of my 30-plus years in franchising, I have worked with many of the best and brightest in the franchise world, some of whom I have had the honor of calling my friends and colleagues at the iFranchise Group. Currently, our 27 consultants have more than 500 years of experience in franchising—much of which has come in senior roles with major brand-name franchise companies.

My good friend and partner at iFranchise Group, Dave Hood, is the former president of Auntie Anne's, has provided me with tremendous firsthand insight into franchise best practices over the decades, and has been a huge influence on this book—and for both, I owe him a profound debt of gratitude. I have also learned an enormous amount from many of the consultants who have worked with me at iFranchise Group. Leonard Swartz has led six different franchise brands in senior-level positions—starting as the COO of Dunkin' Donuts, and later holding senior management positions at Dunhill Staffing,

Snelling & Snelling, Adia Services (now Adecco), PIP Printing, and a franchise division of ITT. Scott Jewett, whom I have the privilege of calling a friend, grew Line-X from its entry into franchising to its sale to a private equity firm after opening more than 700 franchise units. Jerry Wilkerson, who is like a brother to me, stuck with me through thick and thin in the early days, helped introduce me to the franchise world, and showed me the ropes when it was in his best interest to do otherwise. Our partner at TopFire Media, Matthew Jonas, along with Lia Brakel, who heads our marketing department, has helped me transition from the Stone Age in which we grew up into the digital world of modern franchise marketing. Judy Janusz, the Vice President of Operations at iFranchise Group, has provided the leadership and unwavering commitment to quality that allowed us to build this company, not to mention find the time to write this book. To all of them, I owe a debt of thanks that I can never fully repay.

I could write another book on all I have learned from the tremendous team at iFranchise Group. David Omholt, Barry Falcon, Jeff Abbott, Chris Moorhouse, Cynthia Clarkin, Tommy Clark, Darrell Kolinek, Joanna Meiseles, Gary Prenevost, Charlie Weeks, Mike Baum, Hector Ledesma, Bob Moorhouse, Dan Levy, Jim Green, Joe Bargas, Terry Conroy, Keri DesCoteaux, Ann Anderson, and Emiliano Jöcker have all been part of my education—as has my brother John, who, along with Judy Janusz, also assumes the occasional role of keeping me in line. And Mohamed Charafeddine and Ziad Kaddoura, along with their magnificent team at iFranchise MENAT, have done more than provide me with an education on the franchise world outside North America—they have opened their homes and hearts to me.

I owe a special note of thanks to Natalie Lamb, Donna Imbery, Fran Ryan, and Janet Scheuerman, who, in addition to everything else, directly contributed to this book. And I owe a thank you, an apology, and a round of applause to my editor, Jen Dorsey, who in addition to her great work on this book was a huge part of my first book, *Franchise Your Business*, but whom I neglected to formally acknowledge the last time around.

And for everyone else at iFranchise Group who kept things running smoothly so that I was able to devote the time this book required, especially Olivia Carter, Sandy Steele, Judy Palomo, Tonya Hamilton, Cathy Coursey, and Tammy McGrath, thank you.

It has been my distinct privilege and honor to learn from these people, and from the many others—clients, consultants, and lawyers alike—who have shared their franchise insight and experience with me over the years. To thank them all would take another chapter or two. It is my sincere hope that I have been able to impart some small part of the lessons they have taught me in this book.

ABOUT THE AUTHOR

Mark Siebert is the author of *Franchise Your Business: The Guide to Employing the Greatest Growth Strategy Ever* (Entrepreneur Press, 2016). Siebert founded the iFranchise Group in 1998. Since 1984, he has been instrumental in the success of numerous national franchisors. Some of the more prominent companies and organizations he has helped include 1-800-Flowers, Ace Hardware, Anheuser-Busch, Amoco, Armstrong World Industries, The Athlete's Foot, Auntie Anne's, Berlitz, BP Oil, Bridgestone/Firestone, Buffalo Wild Wings, Carstar, Checkers/Rally's, Chem-Dry, Chevron, Circle K, Claire's, Coldwell Banker, Comfort Keepers, Denny's, Einstein Bros. Bagels, El Pollo Loco, FedEx Office, Fidelity Investments, The Goddard School, Guinness, Häagen-Dazs, Hallmark, HoneyBaked Ham, IBM, Jackson Hewitt, John Deere, Krispy Kreme, LA Weight Loss, LensCrafters, Line-X, The Little Gym, Manpower, Massage Envy, McAlister's Deli, Mobil Oil, Nestlé, Nissan (Saudi Arabia),

Oreck, Payless ShoeSource, Perkins, Petland, Pinkberry, Popeyes, PVH, Rita's Italian Ice, Ryder Truck Rental, Sears, Senior Helpers, Shell Oil, Sky Zone, Sonic, Subway, T-Mobile, Texaco, Togo's, and the U.S. Navy.

Siebert serves as a partner and member of the board of directors of TopFire Media, a franchise and consumer media company that specializes in public relations, search engine optimization, social media posting, pay-per-click marketing, and inbound marketing. He also serves as a partner in iFranchise Group International, which oversees licensed operations in the Middle East. Siebert is active in the International Franchise Association (IFA), is a past member of the board of directors of the American Association of Franchisees & Dealers (AAFD), and was a member of the board of directors of i9 Sports (a 140-unit team sports franchisor) during its sale to private equity.

He has presented hundreds of speeches and seminars on franchising in cities around the globe and has been a featured speaker for the IFA, the International Franchise Expo, the IFA's Legal Symposium, the American Bar Association, the National Restaurant Association, and major franchise events in Argentina, Chile, Indonesia, Japan, Mexico, the Philippines, Peru, and Uruguay.

Siebert has also published more than 250 articles in dozens of business and professional periodicals, is the featured columnist for "How to Franchise a Business" for Entrepreneur.com, and regularly writes for *Franchise Times* magazine, Forbes.com, and FranchiseExpo. com. He has been a featured guest on business programs airing on CNN, Fox Business Network, and other networks, both in the U.S. and abroad. He is frequently called upon as an expert witness in franchise-related cases. He was named to the *Franchise Times* list of "20 to Watch" in franchising in 2002, in 2001 was named the AAFD's Supporting Member of the Year, and received the AAFD Special Recognition Award in 2003. In 2011, Siebert was the subject of a feature article in *Restaurant Franchising* entitled "The Franchise Growth Guru."

INDEX